DESIGN FOR RELIGION

DESIGN FOR RELIGION

Toward Ecumenical Education

GABRIEL MORAN

SEARCH PRESS

Inquiries should be sent to the publishers
SEARCH PRESS LIMITED
85 Gloucester Road, London SW7 4SU
and not to the printers.

First published in Great Britain in 1971

© 1970 by Herder and Herder Inc.

ISBN 0 85532 277 2

Printed in Great Britain by
Fletcher & Son Ltd, Norwich

Contents

DESIGN FOR RELIGION

Preface

Two years ago I published a collection of essays on religious education entitled *Vision and Tactics*. At the time, a priest from the Midwest wrote me a letter highly critical of the book. He wanted to know why I did not treat real practical issues like the catechetical material from publishers. I wrote back to him and suggested that he reread page 19 of the book which suggested that the problem of catechetics is that it exists. After saying that a field should not exist it is difficult to get excited about some of the practical problems of the field.

In the same letter I said that I had no intention of writing anything else on religious education. As the "God is Dead" theology found, it is difficult to come up with an encore after a declaration of non-existence. To some extent I am going back on that promise in writing this book. From my own point of view, however, I am trying to move forward into the birth of a new field rather than to revivify an old one. The term "ecumenical education" is an attempt to coin a name for that field. The term has no doubt been used before but not exactly in the sense in which I use it.

Attempts to create and to name a new field are seldom successful. Perhaps if many people are engaged in an inquiry similar to this one, an agreement on terms of description will emerge. At many places in the book, particularly the last chapter, I use religious education where I would prefer to use ecumenical education. This adjustment is necessary to establish points of contact with the present institution but I hope that this book will contribute to some dramatic change in the church's educational involvement for the future.

1. Locating the Crisis

As religious education in the Catholic church faced the 1970's all was not well. Many people would suppose that the situation has become progressively worse during the past ten years. This group includes people on the far right who believe that catechetical changes have been in large part responsible for the break up of the traditional Catholicism they had known. However, it is not only a reactionary element that believes that a catechetical movement has had its day and been found wanting. Many people who placed great hope in catechetical change now suspect that at best it was not worth the effort and at worst it has been a disaster.

The last ten years have been ones of stormy struggle to improve the teaching of religion. The history of the catechetical movement is somewhat similar to the history of the liturgical movement. There was a time when nearly everyone admitted that something was wrong and that things had to be livened up. There was a subsequent time of springtime hope when things seemed to be getting better each day and when salvation seemed to be around the next bend. There is finally today when all kinds of changes have been made but the hoped for results seem swamped by trivia, apathy or confusion.

The thesis of this book is that a great deal of progress has been made but it has not been entirely in the direction that had been expected. The progress has come about in moving from questions in the field of religious education to questioning the field of religious education itself. The claim that this move represents progress might be debated. Halting the business of the field to look at the nature and health of the field will seem to

11

some people recessive. There is certainly a kind of narcissistic concern with defining a discipline which leads nowhere except into labyrinths of language cut off from life. There is another kind of introversion, however, which is concerned with the deepest reality of what is at issue. It looks beyond the cure of symptoms toward the health of the organism. Within this framework, the first step on the road to health could be a kind of sickness, of which Lao-Tzu spoke when he wrote: "The holy man is not sick because his sickness sickens him."[1]

The "crisis" which this chapter refers to is not a crisis *in* religious education but a crisis *of* religious education. The distinction is not a quibble over a preposition. It points to the reason why the word crisis is accurately used here. The term crisis has been trivialized by overuse to refer to any frightening or dangerous set of circumstances. More precise use of the word would restrict it to those occasions when the established premises or first principles of a system are under challenge. What characterizes crisis is not only danger but opportunity; what differentiates crisis is that answers must be given where answers have previously been assumed. "A crisis forces us back to the questions themselves and requires from us either new or old answers, but in any case direct judgments. A crisis becomes a disaster only when we respond to it with preformed judgments, that is, with prejudices. Such an attitude not only sharpens the crisis but makes us forfeit the experience of reality and the opportunity for reflection it provides."[2]

On this basis my use of the word crisis is justified. The existence of the enterprise is what is now in question. Both those who criticize religious education for doing too much and those who are critical of it for doing too little should concern themselves with the *kind* of thing they expect. The right wing of religious education (for example, those who bought the 250,000 Balti-

1. *Tao Tê Ching,* chap. 71.
2. Hannah Arendt, *Between Past and Future* (New York, 1961), pp. 174 f.

more Catechisms last year) are quite clear on what they are trying to do. I think that their aim is fundamentally inconsistent with the nature of education but their premises, aims and instruments are consistent with one another. On the other hand, those who have advocated and initiated changes in religious education have usually not gone far enough in establishing a new set of premises and means. Individual statements and small changes are forced into a prior framework instead of being set upon a new foundation.

This book is an attempt, however sketchily achieved, to present a new framework for religious education or what I will refer to as ecumenical education. In presenting an overall plan I hope at the least to stop the charge that I am against religious education for children and that I think that adult education courses are the church's salvation. That position is a silly and simplistic one which I have never advocated anywhere. Much more importantly, I hope this book will stimulate further contributions from people in education and in theology who should be concerned with the problem but who are strangely silent at the moment.

There are two phenomena of the present that I would like to cite which manifest not only the existence but the nature of the crisis in Catholic religious education. The first is the conflict between, on the one hand, many teachers of religion in Catholic school and CCD and, on the other hand, church authorities and conservative critics. The second phenomenon (sometimes consequential on the first) is the exodus of teachers of religion into other fields. This fact, together with the elimination of religion as a subject of study is what I call the disappearance phenomenon.

The criticism of poor teaching is not a new or surprising phenomenon. The surprising thing is that the criticism of religion teaching over the past decade has seemed to increase in direct proportion to the improvement of teacher training. No one would deny that there are still many incompetent teachers of

13

religion who are thoroughly unprepared for their task. But it is hardly less debatable that teachers are better prepared than ever before and immeasurably more competent than the typical teacher of either 1840 or 1950. Furthermore, it should be noted that the severest criticism is often directed toward the best teachers and that the emotional level of the attack indicates that something more basic than a poorly taught religion class is the object of the attack.

This conflict within Catholicism comes not so much from a difference over the success of what is going on as from an irreconcilable difference about what should go on. The right wing, as I have acknowledged, is quite clear on what it wants and fairly accurate in what it sees as happening. The advocates of change are a little cloudy about their objectives (perhaps necessarily) and not entirely candid about what they are doing. Thus, when the critics of religion teaching charge that orthodox Catholic doctrine is not being taught in classrooms, the attacked teachers hastily reply that it most certainly is. The teachers might reply more helpfully by challenging the assumption that indoctrination of any kind is compatible with anything that should be called education. Of course, if a teacher needs his job or if he believes that he is doing much good through it, he may not wish to engage in argument at this level. Everyone has to make his comprom'ses but preferably they should be intelligent and worthwhile comprom'ses. A religion teacher in the Catholic church today is going to have to compromise but he should be clear on why he is in the work and he should be ready for what will come if he is successful in the work.

Each year a new crop of teachers with their shiny new certificates, M.A.'s and Ph.D.'s go into Catholic institutions to teach religion. They are usually dumbfounded when they are charged with undermining the faith of their students and destroying Catholic tradition They ought to recognize that to a large extent the accusation is valid. They are underminers not mainly because they have failed as teachers but because the educational

14

process itself has that effect upon faith and tradition. Referring to the role Socrates played, Hegel wrote: "Socrates, like all heroes who cause new worlds to rise and inescapably the old ones to disintegrate, was experienced as a destroyer: what he stood for is a new form which breaks through and undermines the existing world." All great teachers of anything have something of that effect. My point of emphasis, however, is that in matters of Catholic faith today one need not be a great teacher; one has only to engage in the educative process at all for this undermining to occur. This fact is obscured in many arguments over the orthodoxy of what is being taught. The more important question is whether the words orthodoxy and education are at all compatible.

I shall come back shortly to this issue of whether it is possible to teach a faith, Christian or otherwise. Before dipping back into the history of that question I would like to advert to the second fact that reveals the crisis of religious education, namely, the disappearance phenomenon. Sometimes the teachers of religion disappear, at other times the subject of the teaching disappears. Many people who come to graduate programs to prepare them to teach religion decide in the course of their studies that they do not wish to go back to teach it. These are not the unsuccessful or uninterested ones; often it is the best qualified ones who disappear from the field. Many people teaching literature or history have degrees in theology and religious education. They generally are glad that they studied religion but it has impelled them to teach something other than religion.

The other part of the disappearance act concerns curriculum. As religion is made more "relevant" it seems to disappear into other fields. What is taught in religion class today may be hardly distinguishable from what transpires in literature or social science class. There is something very peculiar about a field which seems to disappear as it improves. Some teachers use a film or a discussion of current social problems in a desperate effort to get attention and discipline, even if not a well-taught

15

class. However, the widespread tendency to go this route cannot be written off as a rear guard action by poorly prepared teachers who do not know what else to do. It is very often the best prepared teachers who are holding discussions about peace, poverty or pollution. They are hard put to justify how their class can be called a religion class since they practically never discuss God, Christ, church, sacraments or commandments; or when those words come up the references are as likely to be negative as positive. The teachers instinctively feel, however, that not only is this approach the best way for them to teach religion but that it is the only way.

Whether or not these teachers are right in this conviction is not my immediate concern. I am mainly interested here in this development as symptomatic of a deep-seated problem in the field of religious education. Does this conviction which arises from the experience of dedicated teachers have theological and educational foundations? Could it be possible that it is paradoxically true that the best way to teach religion is not to teach religion at all but to teach literature, social science or art in the best way possible? Before anyone enthusiastically embraces this paradox, another consideration should be kept in mind. If religious education is identical without remainder to general education, can one expect the continuance of any church bodies? In reply to this question, of course, another might be asked. Should the aim of religious education be to get practicing church members? These two questions raise the issue of whether there are not two very different processes that go under the single name of religious education.

The last sentence returns me to the previous point on the conflict over what is expected from religious education. I would submit that the contemporary conflict in American Catholicism is only revealing a problem inherent to Christianity. From the second century onward Christianity has always been a faith proclaimed to the world and "transmitted" from generation to generation. The main model of transmission was the preacher announcing the word of God. The authority of the preacher was in the message he spoke and not in the education he had received. The good tidings of Christ were passed from one hand to another over the centuries. Through the scriptures with authorized interpretation read from numerous pulpits, the message of salvation could be heard. There is nothing necessarily wrong with this procedure and there may even be a place for it today. But it has very little to do with education as the word is understood in the twentieth century. It could possibly fit under some umbrella meaning of education but unless the preaching model is subsidiary to a much larger process it will almost certainly be mis-educative.[3]

I would stress the point that the problem of the preaching model is inherent to the nature of Christianity. The problem did not originate from a miscalculation of the modern catechetical movement; nor can the problem be resolved by a slight corrective. Indeed, any complete and immediate answer to the problem would necessarily be suspect. Christianity is an historical religion which involves scriptures, tradition and belief in the significance of selected past events. Christianity has always had a problem in preserving its tradition and the problem of transmission will remain as long as Christianity does. However, the development of general formal education in the twentieth century has made the problem particularly acute. When much of education tended to have an authoritarian character, the church's method of education did not appear glaringly different. Educational developments in this century have revealed the disparity between what the church does and what is today understood to be education.

The problem is most acute today in American Catholicism because of that church's enormous commitment to educational institutions. A heated confrontation is shaping up between the faith that built schools to preserve that faith and the schools

3. See James Michael Lee and Patrick C. Rooney (eds.), *Toward A Future for Religious Education* (Dayton, 1970).

17

which challenge faith in the process of carrying out their educational aim. Catholics should be aware, however, that American Protestantism struggled with the same issue, at least on the theoretical level, earlier in this century. American Catholics might find more help in this Protestant writing than they do in Catholic writing coming from the continent today. The latter writing is for the most part narrowly conceived in the mold of the preacher announcing the word. It is not in touch with the peculiarly educational problems that affect America. There is at least a half century of educational writing and practice that American Catholics can find in their own country. This is not a matter of getting some educational techniques to convey the faith so much as a re-understanding of Christianity through placing it into an educational context. George Albert Coe, writing a half century ago, saw what the impact of education would be on Christianity. He wrote: "The Christian teacher's practical dilemma takes the form: Shall the primary purpose of Christian education be to hand on a religion, or to create a new world?"[4] Why "Christian education" raises this question and what the ramifications are for Christian bodies have never been grasped either by Protestant or Catholic churches.

The crisis of religious education springs from the relationship between the two words, religious and education. It sounds like a truism to say that religious education should come from a solid combination of religion and education, but the statement must be made nevertheless. There seems to be no reason why religion and education could not join in a common effort but a problem has arisen from their premature symbiosis. Hybrids tend to attract either the highly creative or the very undisciplined. Religious education is particularly exposed to the danger of being a combination of two weaknesses. It may attract people who are competent in neither of the two things that they are trying to join. Religious education is a cross breed that did not

4. George A. Coe, *What Is Christian Education* (New York, 1929), p. 29.

originate from two fields of scholarship but from the desire of confessional groups to indoctrinate. People who were neither knowledgeable in religion nor skilled in education have tried to induce children to follow the same path they have taken.

Religious education is a field that must be reborn from a meeting of good educational theory and sound theological study. Such pronouncements are liable to sound pretentious. Those who are old enough to remember the 1920's may have a feeling of *déjà vu*. The claim that the 1970's is the era for the birth or rebirth of religious education does not depend on any brilliant insights of this book or any other books today. The problem to be dealt with here is as old as Christianity itself and very few new answers are given to such old problems. But the present age is genuinely novel in two important aspects that are pertinent here. The first novelty is theological, the second is educational.

The church for the first time in its history is in the painful process of developing an ecumenical theology. The word ecumenical does not refer merely to Protestant-Catholic cooperation but to the encounter of Christianity with all forms of religion and non-religion. This context involves not a widening of perspective but a change in the meaning of Christianity itself. From the time of St. Paul's strictures on the Jews and the Greeks, Christianity had defined itself against the other. It is easy to define oneself by saying what one is against; it is even easier to say who one is against. However, the task of Christianity in the last part of this century is to cooperate with others in searching for a truth that is greater than what anyone possesses. Today, practically everyone who has been brought up in the Christian churches carries the remnants of a very unecumenical attitude. But worldwide communication will soon make such an attitude untenable.

An ecumenical theology will have enormous implications for religious education. The relation between the words Christian and religious, which always fluctuates uncertainly in educational discussions, must be carefully explored in this new light. The

19

concern with other faiths will not just add to the curriculum; it will change the method of approach to Christianity. An ecumenical theology will finally break the hold of a preacher model on religious education. Such a theology will encourage or even force education to deal with issues deeper than the teaching of scripture and doctrine.

The other novel factor that will confront us in the last part of the twentieth century is a new educational structure. The change here may be less dramatic because it is spread over a longer period of time. The developments in American education that went under the title of progressivism go back more than seventy-five years. Nevertheless, throughout much of the last twenty-five years many people were willing to write the death notice of this movement. What seems clear now is that the lull was only the prelude to larger changes in education. Reform movements that could not succeed in an earlier day are now becoming both possible and necessary. Man's capability of controlling environments and understanding man are making educational revolutions possible. And the staggering acceleration of political and social change makes large scale educational change urgently necessary.

I would maintain, therefore, that religion and education are ready to form a coalition. Furthermore, this cooperation is a genuinely new development in the history of Christianity. Until now a coalition has not been possible because of deficiencies on one side or the other. Before this century the deficiency was more obviously on the side of education. As education improved the center of the difficulty seemed to shift to religion. The religious education movement in American Protestantism was strong on education but it found little cooperation from the theological side. One should carefully note that it was not theology which led to a preaching model of religious education but a particular kind of theology that did so. The neo-orthodox theology of Barth or Brunner was not very helpful to people looking for theological support in religious education. But a new and chastened liberal theology, functioning in a fully ecumenical context, will find it easy to cooperate with education. As I have already indicated, however, such a theology does not come about without shaking the foundations of Christian faith.

An approach to religious education from the side of religion or theology does not inevitably lead to a preaching model. Conversely, an approach from the side of education does not necessarily avoid it. In fact, those who are approaching religious education today from the educational side are very susceptible to it. They speak of devising the education method that would be sufficient to teach the content of Christian faith. By assuming that Christian theology is to supply them the content, they are unwittingly following the pattern proposed by neo-orthodoxy, namely, that education is to find the techniques for getting across the word of God.

It would be fairly simple if the relationship between theology and education were one in which the former supplied the *content* and the latter dealt with the *method*. Those who are approaching the question from the educational side tend to accept this division of labor. One would think that a division into content and method would be challenged from within educational circles. At any rate, the assumption that theology supplies content and education provides method has been exploded from within theology itself. Theology is as concerned with how men think of God as what they think of him. Theology's contribution is not to supply some data but to engage in a cooperative reflection on the human process. Theologians, even for the sake of theology, ought to have some awareness of what is going on in education. On the other side, educationalists must get something more than a naive grasp upon theology if they are going to contribute to the refounding of religious education. Those in education interested in the teaching of religion cannot pick up their body of teaching material from scripture, theology or anywhere else. At least they cannot do so until they become familiar with the main changes occurring in theological method.

21

I am not suggesting that people must be experts in both education and religion to make a contribution. But I am insisting that there be enough awareness of the other pole of the relation so that the relationship is not conceived of in a simplistic way. To help a dialogue between those in theology and those in education there should perhaps be those who risk building bridges. They are in danger of becoming hybrids who are competent in neither of the two things they are supposedly joining. Being aware of this danger is at least a partial protection against it. As long as one has some solid footing somewhere, forays beyond the boundary of one's specialty need not be disastrous.

The proposal I am making would seem to be a fairly simple one, almost too obvious for saying. Yet the proposal to re-establish religious education as a combination of good religion and sound education meets with great resistance. Most administrators of the present field have a vested interest in seeing it continue essentially as it is. Textbook makers, for example, have a high financial stake in the present field. Many people associated with religious education are insecure in both theological and educational circles. They prefer to carve out a field different from theology and education which, if somewhat thin, is at least one in which they are comfortable. Occasional cries for more research in religious education must be regarded with suspicion. Research in theology and research in education are no doubt worthwhile ventures. Before one engages in research in religious education one would like some assurance that the field exists and that the research problems are not the creations of a pseudo-discipline to perpetuate itself.

Borrowing from both religion and education, I would like to set forth in the following chapters a total pattern of religious or ecumenical education. In Chapter 2, I summarize some themes of contemporary theology, particularly the relation between the terms Christian and religious. The third chapter contains some general principles of education. This chapter describes man's powers of learning in the context of the social structure he is called to change. Chapter 4 combines the material from the preceding two chapters to produce a total framework for religious education. Chapters 5 and 6 fill out in detail this over-all plan; the former deals with religious education for the pre-adult, the latter deals with an adult model of maturity and the relation of Christian faith to it. The seventh and last chapter suggests some institutional changes in the Catholic church on the basis of the preceding six chapters.

The pattern which emerges from this coalition of religion and education is a model which is in continuity with the past but totally transforms it. Herbert McCabe writes: "A revolution is never intelligible in terms of the society it supersedes; but that society must be intelligible in terms of the revolution. Adult life cannot be understood in terms of childhood, but it is part of maturity to understand and accept one's childhood."[5] The phrase which I have used to characterize the new model of religious education is "adult centered" and the choice of this phrase is not unconnected to McCabe's example in the above quotation. The task is always to understand the whole but the whole cannot at once be understood and thus one must look for categories that are both comprehensive and able to bear distinction. My choice of the phrase adult centered indicates a starting point, a focus and an aim in understanding the whole process. Perhaps the phrase cannot bear all of this weight and I would be willing to try other terms. In any case, my use of the phrase refers to what I see as the main direction of both theology and education and the point at which they converge. I advocate adult centeredness in religious education because I take this to be the main point of theology. Likewise, adult centered religious education follows from the fact that all education ought to shift in that direction.

I have constantly used phrases such as adult oriented, adult centered, adult directed to distinguish what I am talking about from "adult education." The change I am advocating is not the

5. Herbert McCabe, *What Is Ethics All About?* (Washington, 1969), p. 27.

offering of adult education courses in addition to or in substitution for courses given to children. Rather, I am talking about an overall change in the process. If education were directed to adulthood, presumably there would be an expansion in course offerings for adults, but that is not the essence of what is at issue. In fact, the addition of adult education courses done in isolation from any other educational changes would run counter to the need for adult centered education. Adding more courses might only bolster the myth that the way to prepare for life is to take courses. Going to school for an interminable number of years will never prepare anyone to step forth into something else called real life. Adult centered education would always be engaged in further penetrating the experience of life that is already available.

One can gather from the above paragraph that an adult centered education is one that is by the same reasoning experience centered. Indeed, the two phrases are almost interchangeable. The latter phrase, experience centered, may seem preferable as being more self-explanatory. Actually, however, experience centered is not so obvious in meaning as some people would suppose and by using adult centered in conjunction with it I would hope to clarify both phrases.

The category of experience is a continuing theme throughout the following pages. I shall deal most directly with it in chapter three. Here I wish only to note that experience has been at the center of educational discussion in America throughout the century. But talking about an experience centered education is not an answer to the problem; at best it is a small step toward defining a proper approach. Recently, C. Ellis Nelson, head of Union Theological Seminary's Religious Education Department, visited Catholic catechetical centers throughout Europe. On his return to this country he wrote a paper which pointed out that nearly everywhere he went, the stress was on experience centered learning. The question he asks in his essay is: "What functions as the authority in Roman Catholicism if education becomes experience centered?" The question is a legitimate and important one. I think that there is an answer to the question but it is not easily come by.

It would be somewhat dishonest and ultimately self-defeating to pretend that experience centered education does not conflict with much of Christianity's past and present. One would suspect that despite all the recent talk about experience in Catholic and Protestant religious education, the education does not in fact center there. On the one hand, experience is short-circuited sooner or later (usually sooner) by the introduction of material removed from the child's experience. On the other hand, the experience of the student is used as a jumping off point to teach the bible and Christian doctrine. In both cases, experience is trivialized to such an extent that to call this approach experience centered is inaccurate.

The main problem here is not whether experience might on occasion seem to contradict some point of Christian belief. It is a question of principle: What takes precedence, experience or set forms of beliefs? Carl Rogers, the great American psychologist, describes this question arising in his own life. He became convinced that in order to follow experience he had to give up the theological study he had been pursuing.[6] People in the field of religious education who speak glibly of experience centered education often present little evidence that they have agonized over this question or indeed understood the question at all. If the question can be answered, it will require considerable rethinking of the nature of Christianity and the function of bible and doctrine in the Christian churches. It is not at all clear that this theological revolution has occurred in the minds of many people trying to change religious education.

The problem of combining experience centered education with Christian belief is one inherent to Christianity itself. Liberal forms of Protestantism have been able to soften the conflict by

6. Carl Rogers, *On Becoming a Person* (Boston, 1961), p. 8.

their approach to Christian doctrine. But Roman Catholicism would at first sight seem to have an insurmountable problem. As Harrison Elliot realized in his advocacy of an experience centered education in Protestantism: "An experience-centered educational process is inconsistent, however, with positions dogmatically and finally held. This is the source of much of the opposition to religious education and is also the source of the conflict within education itself. There has often been a tendency for each religious faith to consider its own the only true religion. This results not only in the unwillingness to learn from other faiths, but also in the practice of branding them as false and untrue."[7]

Christianity, and Catholicism in particular, has become more tolerant in recent years or at least less condemnatory which may be a different thing. The achievement of a truly tolerant position that asserts the truth as it sees it, while listening to the truth that the other sees, is still in the making. A true tolerance requires not an adjustment of some theological positions but a new development of theology from an ecumenical starting point. Until this ecumenical theology comes to exist in the churches there will not be experience centered education there.

A few further comments must be made about the word ecumenical in the subtitle of this work. There are two dist'nct but related meanings that are contained in the word. Ecumenical education refers to a study of the religions of mankind. If one religion is made the particular object of study, the study of that religion should be carried out within this larger framework. It is not unecumenical to study one religion so long as there is relation to and comparison with other religions. Ecumenical education would include more than an attitude of mind although the right attitude is a prerequisite to other changes in an ecumenical movement.

The term ecumenical movement originally referred to in-

7. Harrison Elliot, *Can Religious Education Be Christian?* (New York, 1940), p. 317.

tramural changes in Protestantism. At a later stage it became a Protestant-Catholic concern, at which point the word ecumenism seemed to gain prominence. From there Christian leaders were anxious to include Jews in the conversation. This stage has been successful in some places although many Jewish leaders, for their own good reason, are not overly anxious to have this Christian embrace. The ecumenical movement is for many Jews still an intramurally Christian affair. Despite the limited success of Christian-Jewish dialogue, or perhaps spurred by the difficulties of it, Christian leaders in recent years have looked to a wider ecumenism. In relation to this ecumenism everything else up to now has been merely preparatory. We will finally have what with accuracy can be called an ecumenical or world movement. Within this conversation Christianity will cease to be the dominant partner that dictates all the terms of the dialogue. It is a breathtaking new step which does not obliterate the Christian past but which does reverse much of its meaning.

The other related sense of the word ecumenical pertains directly to its etymology. An ecumenical education is one that will be concerned with the world man lives in. Much of education, both general and religious, has tended to cut off man from his roots in nature and his involvement with the structures of this material world. To write about ecumenical education in this sense is to write about all education or to advocate a particular way of carrying out all education. Obviously, I cannot deal with all education but my remarks about religion in education are drawn from principles of general education and in turn have implications for the general notion of education. These two meanings of ecumenical are not related entirely by accident. Christianity's encounter with the world religions is at once a meeting with the world and the religions. As Christianity considers other religions it will also be forced to reconsider the relation of man to the world, person to nature and the organism to the environment. The reason for this dynamism will be discussed in the next chapter.

I would judge this book to be successful if it caused some people to read further in theology and/or education as their own step toward the rebirth of religious education. No one person can complete the task nor even can this generation complete it but it is up to this generation to take the first decisive steps. Writing forty years ago, Coe could see that "the now-rising generation in the churches has been born into a happily unhappy situation: happy because of the unprecedented amount of thought that Christians are giving to Christian education, unhappy because the farther we Christians go with this thinking the farther away seem the solutions for our problems. I refer, not to our discovery of the mountainous inertia of both ministers and laity; not to the superficiality of much religious education that intends to be progressive; not even to the baffling problem of how to secure trained teachers, but to difficulties that are inherent in the very idea of Christian education."[8]

The one misjudgment of Coe's in the above statement was his supposition that there were many other people who had the same vision he did. There probably are still only a limited number of people who grasp the problem inherent to a Christian education. But the theological and educational changes have been occurring with accelerated pace and they are bound to cause dramatic changes in the churches. What could successfully be avoided forty years ago is becoming more difficult to sidestep today. One need not be cynical to say that in the Catholic church the one irresistible pressure for change will probably be a financial one. When that does come about it is to be hoped that the large-scale changes will be based upon some consistent positions in theology and education.

8. Coe, *op. cit.,* p. 183.

2. Religious, Christian and Ecumenical

ANY attempt to deal with the question of religious education must at the same time be an attempt to understand the great religious and theological issues of our time. Some educational approaches to religious education seem to assume that the religious material to be taught is generally agreed upon and is located somewhere in some books. This assumption runs counter to a general educational principle, namely, that the field in question must be thoroughly understood by those who set educational directions for it. More importantly, there is a peculiar difficulty in religious education by reason of the term religious. When one refers to education in religion, there are some ambiguities and complexities that set off the problem of its teaching from that of physics, mathematics or American history. The difficulties refer not to the differing theories within the field nor to peripheral disagreements about its conclusions but to the existence, meaning and nature of religion itself.

In this chapter I would like to sort out some of the theological problems connected with religious education. To a large extent my procedure will be one of pointing out the ambiguous meaning of the word religious. Instead of doing away with the ambiguity by a clear definition, I will try to preserve the ambiguity of the word while trying to reduce the confusion level built into ambiguity. This strategy seems to me the most preferable one, given the historical and current usage of the word religion together with my suspicion that this extraordinary span of meaning for the word religion is the result of accurately perceiving the ambiguity built into reality itself.

Some of the problems with the word religion can be immediately seen by comparing it to two closely related words: church and Christianity. These two relations, namely, religion vs. church and religion vs. Christianity, are themselves in turn related. A preliminary exposition about these relationships may be helpful at this point.

The notion of church is obviously distinguishable from religion but it is amazing how far the language of the "Christian West" has gone in identifying the two of them. Unless a Christian in this country has consciously worked out a distinction for himself, he will almost inevitably assume that church and religion cover approximately the same ground. There is a genuine truth at stake here, namely, that religion always manifests itself in a communal, social or institutional form that the Christian calls church; but it is a truth which has been repeated a little too glibly, particularly by Roman Catholics. The statement that the church embodies religion cannot be converted into the statement that religion is embodied in church, adequately and without constriction. At the least it must be said that the relationship between religion and church is more complex than that of contained to container. It could be maintained that church, like any social body, is inevitably suppressive of some religious elements. These elements are likely to show up somewhere other than in what anyone would call a church.

I wish to make clear that I am not attacking the contemporary church in referring to it with words like constrictive or suppressive. On the contrary, I am trying to obviate some of the attacks by insisting on the distinction between religion and church. People who were once triumphalistic toward the church are those most susceptible to making vitriolic attacks against the church. Their cast of mind has altered very little; in both stages there is a refusal to accept the fact that the church is a human institution with all the foibles that mankind is heir to. Recent fumings against the "institutional church" are at best ill stated. Presumably the phrase could be a shorthand redundancy to refer to the operational patterns in the church institution that need drastic change. More often, one suspects, "institutional church" is being contrasted to some other vague conception which logically would have to be a non-institutional church. It is not enough to say that this latter does not and cannot exist; it must be said with urgency that to defend freedom, truth or person-hood by appeal to the nonexistent only exposes these values to worse treatment at the hands of the powers that do exist. In this connection I would like to stress that my contrast of religion and church does not presume that religion here refers only to the inner world, the private sphere or the solitary individual. Religion does exist in personal, material and institutional forms that may not be identical with the existing church.

The "decline of religion" has been discussed *ad nauseam* during the past decade not only in theological journals but in popular literature and news media. Sociologists have often commented that it would be helpful to try to distinguish the religious problems from the church problems. The instinctive reaction of many Christians to this suggestion is that the two are so closely tied together that a problem of church is a prob-lem of religion and vice versa. I have admitted that there is a real insight in that conviction but it does not eliminate the need for the distinction. Without the distinction there is no way to track down the church's problems except to attribute them to communism, secularism, atheism, paganism, etc. These great forces may be real enemies of the church but one should not immediately jump to that level of explanation. We should first take a simple look at the human forms in which the church exists, forms which may not be serving the church any longer and may be causing failures that are not anyone's fault.

Much of what is called a religious crisis today would be more accurately designated an ecclesiastical crisis. The criteria for the judgment of a crisis, for example, church attendance, seminary size, financial contributions, are almost exclusively church measurements. The difficulties of measuring "religiosity" as dis-tinct from "churchiness" do constitute a great problem for

31

sociology. The result in history was a gradual shift in the sociology of religion from the study of religion to the study of church.[1]

It would be a help if we could see that there is always some lack of congruence between religion and the existing form of church. It would be particularly helpful for us to recognize that recent times have speeded up the pace of the need to adapt for congruence. "Under conditions of rapid social change the problem becomes still more acute. The everyday concerns of the fathers are no longer those of the sons and many of the concerns of the sons were unknown to the fathers . . . A serious problem of institutional specialization of religion consists, therefore, in the fact that the 'official' model of religion changes at a slower rate than the 'objective' social conditions that codetermine the predominant individual systems of 'ultimate' significance."[2]

The distinction between a religious crisis and a church crisis would be a help in understanding some educational issues. The supposed crisis in religious education may be in more precise terms a crisis in church education. The term church education in this context refers specifically to a process of education in how to be a practicing member of a church body. As one would rightfully expect, most of the education sponsored by Catholic and Protestant churches falls into this category. When education by the church does become religious exploration it is likely to set up a tension if not outright conflict with the existing churches. The criticism of the church by teachers and students can easily be naive or unfair. It remains true, nonetheless, that some of the crisis of church education may be traceable in part to the success of religious education. Ironically, therefore, some of the church's problems are brought on by the successful part of the education which the church sponsors. It should also be added that there may be a great deal of informal religious edu-

1. See Peter Berger, *Rumor of Angels* (Garden City, 1969); Thomas Luckmann, *The Invisible Religion* (New York, 1967).
2. Luckmann, *op. cit.,* pp. 82 f.

cation taking place outside of and sometimes in conflict with the churches.

The second difficulty with the word religion lies in its relation to the word Christianity. This problem is obviously related to the previous analysis but the connection is a complex one. In looking at the relation of Christian and religious I am going to shift away from the institutional problems of Christianity toward its ecumenical problem vis-à-vis other religions. In this case, too, the relation is not summed up by a yes or no but must be worked out as a dialectic without final answer.

Christian theology up to the present has been a provincial study carried out within a narrow cultural setting. It will generally continue to function inside these narrow confines for a long while simply because a worldwide perspective cannot be had by willing it. Christian theology, however, can begin preparing itself for some future integration by shifting its attitudes. The preconditions for dialogue with the East may still be in the building stage but to care about dialogue is already a preverbal dialogue. In time the situating of Christianity on the stage of the world's religions will bring about a revolution in theological method. "It will be just as inconceivable for a theologian to construct his system without the worldwide community in mind as it would be for him to 'construct' an intellectual position unaware that Aristotle has thought about the world or that existentialists have raised new orientations, or unaware that the earth is a minor planet in a galaxy that is vast only by terrestrial standards."[3]

Christians of the West, whether they will it or not, are going to have to confront other religious traditions. Before Christians can judge other faiths they will have to come to an appreciation of each concrete religious tradition. The general condemnation of religion in recent Christian theology can only be called scandalous. Faced with what seemed to be a crisis of religion, some theologians found too easy an escape in dissociating Chris-

3. Del Byron Schneider, *No God But God* (Minneapolis, 1969), p. 123.

tianity from religion. The logic that opposed secular to religious and then put Christianity on the side of the secular was inaccurate and could not be sustained. The words religious and secular are not so clear in meaning as is often presumed: it is not even evident that they should be opposed to each other. Furthermore, the relation of Christianity to religion is not a simple one. As a start we must at least make a distinction between the general category of religion and particular existing religions.

Before trying to work through this question theologically, I would like to point out that this theological problem has hovered in the background of religious education. Seldom has the problem been directly dealt with in religious education. The term Christian education has been much more common in Protestant than in Catholic circles. At times there have been attempts to work out the relation between Christian education and religious education but not with entire success since the whole theological issue has been sidestepped.[4]

When the currency of the word religious began to decline in value more emphasis was placed upon Christian education and the term became more popular in Catholic circles. Recently, however, the term religion, particularly in the context of university education, has been regaining in value. The phrase religious education begins to sound respectable again. Perhaps the time is opportune for setting out a more consistent use of the words which will be based upon a firm theological position. It is easy to be biased about the comprehensiveness of one's own historical vantage point. Nonetheless, I would like to hope that there is a more balanced view today concerning the relation of Christian and religious than was available in the past.

The relationship between Christian and religious could conceivably fall into one of three categories: 1) Christianity could

4. See D. Campbell Wyckoff, "Toward a Definition of Religious Education as a Discipline," in *Religious Education,* 62 (Sept./Oct., 1967), pp. 387–394.

be a species of the genre religion 2) Christianity could be a negation of what constitutes religion 3) Christianity could be dialectically related to religion, affirming one part of its meaning and negating another. The thesis of this chapter is that the answer lies somewhere within the third of these possibilities. In this regard, two points should be noted immediately. First, Christianity may be dialectically related to religion generically and abstractly conceived; so may other religions like Hinduism or Taoism. Second, the process of affirming/negating does not necessarily imply that part of religion is bad and part is good. If it were that simple, one could sort out the good meaning from the bad and give each a different name. But the process is more complicated in a dialectic in which the negating is an inner moment of the affirmation. What is negated is not the bad but the primitive stages that must be transcended. What is proper for a child may be quite inadequate for an adult. Not that the child can be entirely left behind but what is of the child must be given a larger context in the life of an adult. In this sense the childish in the adult must be negated in order that the childlike may flourish. On the other hand, there is nothing wrong with being childish so long as one is a child.

I use the word religion with two quite different meanings. The ambiguity is not the result of logical confusion but of the real ambiguity in human life. In the first place, religion pertains to the attitudes of primitives and children. Religion in this sense is pre-scientific and tied to fanciful, nonrational stories about the gods dealing with the world. Such religion, particularly because of the terrors of the universe, always borders on the magical, that is, there is a strong tendency to look for mechanisms to control the gods. In such a process, the myths turn into mythology, the will of the gods becomes expansively codified and the rites become totems and taboos.

The great religions of the world have all reacted against this very natural tendency. Christian theologians have claimed that Christianity goes the farthest in purifying and transforming these religious tendencies. I will refrain in this book from trying to prove that Christianity does it best and I will concentrate on what Christianity has done and can do well. As stressed in recent Christian theology, Christianity found itself at odds with much of the religion current at the time of Jesus and the apostolic church. Christian beliefs such as creation, incarnation and salvation held important implications for man's attitude toward nature, human individuals and empirical science. In consort with other developments in the West, Christianity helped to unleash human capacities for experimental and mathematical science and the development of technology. In doing so, Christianity, without clearly intending it, helped to "depopulate the heavens"; all nature became exposed to man's touch.

Insofar as human powers were released and perfected, this development of the modern period must certainly be counted as gain. But there is a history of forgetting as well as discovery and one may not be richer for all one's discoveries. The adult who forgets that he was once a child, and indeed still has the childlike within him, is older but not much wiser than he was as a child. The celebrated phrase of Dietrich Bonhoeffer that the world has "come of age" does not mean that men today are necessarily stronger, better and wiser. Surely, Bonhoeffer, who coined the phrase while waiting for death in a concentration camp, was aware of that fact.

There are many disagreements about the effect of Christianity on the development of the West. However, it seems fairly clear that Christianity did give encouragement to the use of human reason for discovering answers rather than accepting religious myths. This fact must not be extended to suggest that Christianity is concerned with reason rather than feeling, science rather than myth, individual freedom rather than nature. Christianity at its best has been understood to be concerned with all things human and divine in such a way that all things genuinely human could be included within it. Religious practices that Christianity found itself in opposition to could not be accepted as ultimately true but neither should they have been presumed to be totally false. If these practices reflect real human concerns, in however distorted a fashion, a hearing must be given to them. Throughout its history Christianity has in fact borrowed modes of expression current to the time. Although its attitude has at times been narrowly polemical, it has also practiced a more positive approach.

A case in point was brought out by Hugo Rahner in tracing the early church's attitude to the mystery religions.[5] Rahner showed that the early church strongly opposed the mystery religions when the latter was a strong competitor with Christianity. At the moment when Christianity might have been expected to be pronouncing a death warrant over the mystery rites, it changed its attitude. The Christian church then went on to embrace many of the forms and elements of the mystery religions. As soon as it was clear that the mysteries were not the final truth it was possible to embrace them as the embodiment of some human truth.

Christianity, as a force exploding out from the category of religion, undercut religious answers and let loose the nonreligious elements of life. But Christianity, from the start and of necessity, is itself a particular religion with all the limitations of anything that is particular. Even if one should claim that it is the best of religions, it would still be only the best one and not the totality of what is human. Unless Christianity is in turn affirmed/negated by being lifted out of itself and beyond itself, its strength and greatness will be corruptive. The religion that has the most exalted idea of god can easily become the one with the most degraded idea of man. Christianity, if it is to be true to itself, must always be pushing beyond its own truth to some greater truth yet to be born. The historical forms of Christianity have not satisfied and cannot satisfy the deepest cravings and sublimest attitudes of man. Christianity has a right to

5. Hugo Rahner, *Greek Myth and Christian Mystery* (New York, 1963).

chasten and purify religion so long as it is willing to be chastened and purified in return.

Beyond the two stages that I have so far described, namely, the primitive religious stage and a narrowly Christian stage, there is a third stage. I would call this stage the ecumenical era of religion/Christianity. It would be misleading to call this stage post-Christian since I am not positing that Christianity disappears or that one must cease to be a Christian in order to be ecumenically religious. On the contrary, I am suggesting that not only does Christianity continue but that the religious elements which Christianity helped to undercut and discredit re-emerge in a new synthesis. The result is not an esperanto religion that is artificially constructed but an ecumenical stance within particular religious traditions that are deeply rooted in the human. The dream of the "age of the spirit" that has haunted much of the West since the twelfth century was not without a basis; but the spirit can not be an anti-institutional one. If the third age really synthesizes the preceding two, it will not claim to leave behind particular institutional forms. The religious life of man will never cease to be material, social and rooted in a stream of history.

The three stages of religious, Christian and ecumenically religious/Christian can be exemplified by considering the function of revelation in each.[6] In the first stage a religion has a revelation. The content of the revelation may range from the trivial to the profound, but the important thing is that the gods have bequeathed certain rites, beliefs and codes to men. At its best such a religious revelation can provoke wonder, adoration, and ecstasy. At its worst such revelations engender fear, terror and submission. No matter how beautiful the message of the gods may be it is a pronouncement which calls man not to

6. See: *Theology of Revelation* (New York, 1966); "The God of Revelation" in *God, Jesus, Spirit* (New York, 1969), pp. 3–15; *Experiences in Community* (New York, 1968), pp. 72–76.

reason but to obey. To submit, whether it be from awe-struck joy or craven fear, is in the long run not a very healthy human attitude. The pre-rational must some day come to terms with the light of critical reason.

The biblical religion of Judaism and Christianity also has a notion of revelation, although the word seldom appears in the Hebrew scriptures. For most of the history of Christian theology the term was also presumed and not directly commented upon. When the word did become central in modern times, Christianity was more intent upon settling into the category of religion rather than exploding it forward. Not surprisingly, therefore, the modern use of revelation in Christian theology has remarkable similarities to the primitive use, that is, revelation is conceived of as a message from god. The one striking difference with the "Christian revelation" was that it had become a very reasonable matter. Prophecy, miracle and mystery could now be neatly composed into a syllogism that deposits one in the arms of mother church or her ministers. To refer to a "Christian revelation" almost unavoidably implies that there is a revelation which is specifically Christian and possessed by no one but the Christian church. It is not by accident that this position has led to intolerance, authoritarianism and social ineffectiveness.

Fortunately, there has always been more to Christianity than its theology manuals and its official stances. Another meaning of revelation was implicit in the Hebrew bible and never entirely lost in the development of Christianity. This meaning of revelation has become more prominent in the twentieth century through the combined pressures of biblical study, human sciences, social calamity and the ecumenical movement. The distinctive thing about Judaism was that the Jews did not have oracles from their god handed down at the beginning of time. The Jews claimed to meet God in their own historical experience. They did not have a revelation, they were engaged in one.

Martin Buber's "No one is so possessed as he who thinks that he possesses God" portrays the Jewish attitude toward anyone claiming that he possesses a revelation from God.

Judaism thus released men from bondage to the gods; it punched a hole in the sky. Henceforth, there was only one God to be believed in and he was not the Jewish god but the God of mankind. A God who has involved himself in partnership with all men is revealed wherever there are men. Every act of revealing is a revealing of the divine and human in indissoluble relationship. Whenever a person truly sees the face of another man he implicitly sees all mankind and has intimations of what surpasses all understanding.

Christianity, when it has been true both to its Jewish roots and to its prophetic founder, Jesus of Nazareth, has talked less of the revelation it had and concentrated more on the revelation it was to be. At least Christianity was to be a means of revealing aspects of the divine and human that might otherwise be missed. Wherever men have put their lives on the line for the ideals of Christ's gospel, a revelation of God has always been apparent. But because of the limited framework in which Christianity has grown up, it has always been exposed to the error of presuming that it had a Christian revelation, that is, a set of revealed truths which was the church's possession.

In previous writing on this subject I have pointed out that phrases like "Christian revelation" and "revealed truth" are misleading and ought to be avoided. Obviously, one can stretch the meaning of terms and give these phrases a legitimate meaning. However, the phrases are laden with meanings that are symptomatic of such a fundamentally wrong notion of revelation that the phrases must be challenged. The direct object of the word reveal would be most precisely God/man. In some sense, all truths can be said to be revealed by God but precisely in that sense it is *all* truth that is revealed and not some truths which are revealed as opposed to other nonrevealed truths. The Christian may claim that there are truths in his bible and church tradition which are more revealing than other truths but it is illogical to say that these truths are revealed and that the others are not.

The issue here is not a quibbling over the extension of a word. Whether the divine is conceived of as ever being a substitute for the human is crucial to ecumenism, tolerance and freedom. The premise of Judaism and Christianity is that the divine is always being manifested in the human. The medium is everything and the consequence is worlds yet to be created. To give up the language of "revealed truths" and "Christian revelation" does not make the tradition become vague or misty; it is as clear as ever. What does happen is that Christianity is set squarely within the context of a world history where Christians must search for the truth with everyone else.

Letting go of one's divinely revealed truths is a frightening experience, as indeed it is supposed to be. But it is a cause of panic only to those who are so rational and dominative that they cannot imagine any other way of being in the world except to possess and control. It would be interesting to speculate on the connection between this revelation theory and an overly masculinized church. I suspect that if there had been women theologians in sufficient number a different route would have been followed.

In the third stage revealed truths and Christian revelation no longer make sense but truth and Christianity by no means disappear. Most of all, the notion of revelation becomes richer and broader than ever before. Revelation is a concept that must be filled in from the phenomenology of human relationship and the comparison of religions. Both of these tasks have hardly been begun because neither can be taken seriously until the prior position of revealed truths is relinquished.

The question for Christianity now is how it can contribute to the revelation of God/man. Although it is false to say that the church has a revelation, it may be possible to say that the revelation has a church. What I mean is that revelation is not a vague, philosophical generality nor a misty, spiritual experience but a divine-human relationship that is concretely expressed in social forms. Christianity would not be less important or less necessary than in the second stage. It would be at least one of the necessary embodiments of man's permanent religious quest. Christianity has bigger worlds to face but first it must give up its ecclesio-central world. Like an adolescent clutching desperately at the truths that it possesses, it must learn to relax and grow into a world of mutuality where one's identity is preserved in the acceptance of a world that does not center on oneself.

We are not caught, therefore, between the alternatives of a fierce and uncritical religiousness on the one hand or a watered down Christianity without God, Christ, sin or scripture on the other hand. Early in his book, *The Future of Belief,* Leslie Dewart remarks that the church ought to realize it has a mission instead of a message.[7] I gather the point he is trying to make but the juxtaposition he uses is not very helpful. The main problem is not that the church thought it had a message but that it forgot that the message was its own. The church's message is the church's and not God's. At least any message, ecclesiastical or otherwise, cannot be simply identified with God. The church ought to keep offering what message it has but it should not be surprised if most people are uninterested and it certainly should not condemn those people who do not accept its message. Perhaps those people have a few messages of their own which seem to be making sense and which the church might learn something from. There is a quite definite message of Christianity and it is neither more nor less than an interpretation of the whole of experience. "It can be argued that if we surrender the notion that we are merely the passive channel of divine commands, then we have the courage to express our judgments, and if we make mistakes, as we always have and always will, then we will have the courage to change our judgments. The church then would see itself as speaking and acting *before* God and it

7. Leslie Dewart, *Future of Belief* (New York, 1966), p. 8.

would accept the responsibility for its actions. What it would cease to do is to attempt to avoid this responsibility by claiming to speak *for* God."[8]

There is no need for Christianity to give up its message, its symbolism, its doctrine or its rites. In fact, there is considerable reason today to doubt that the church should align itself with the rational forces that oppose all semblance of myth, wonder, nature and fantasy. A. N. Whitehead once remarked that "the common sense of the eighteenth century acted on the world like a bath of moral cleansing . . . but if men cannot live on bread alone, still less can they do so on disinfectants." There is a realignment occurring today in which forces that had seemed to be deadly enemies are forming at least temporary coalitions. Marxist-Christian conversation is only one example, and perhaps not the most significant one, of such reshuffling. There is a growing suspicion today of any monodimensional approach to man's problems. Thus, concerning technology it is no longer possible to be uncritically for it and it is naive or irresponsible to be simply against it. What is needed is a coalition of people who will strive to place technology at the service of worldwide human improvement. Similarly, with regard to religion, we are no longer in need of polemics either for or against it. We do need a wide spectrum of people cutting across many traditional boundaries who appreciate what religion has meant in the past and can intelligently criticize it in the present.

Correlated with the move into a third stage of ecumenical religion/Christianity is a new attitude toward nature. In the primitive religious stage man was subject to nature and nature was subject to the gods. In the narrowly Christian stage, man and nature switched positions so that man was now the dominant one. In the ecumenical stage man will turn back to nature not to be subjugated again but to enter into a respectful and loving exchange with it. Conservationists have usually missed the point

8. Eugene Fontinell, *Toward A Reconstruction of Religion* (Garden City, 1970), p. 160.

in trying to preserve the land untouched instead of working to have the land dealt with in intelligent fashion. "Man, the willing man, has to strive toward order. This is his obligation. Although each of us is not entitled to use the earth as his altar, we have to deal with it with the same respect, since nature preceded and may well outlive man. As visitors of this world, we have to show much greater reverence when we touch it."[9]

There will be a temptation in Christian theology to turn away from man and go back to nature, but this move is not possible and it would be a wrong path even if it were possible. Anthropomorphism has never been the fault of theology. The fault lies rather in the images of man which either excluded his relation to nature or cast him only in the role of nature's subduer. If Christian theology will be attentive both to other religions and to a variety of nonreligious approaches to this question, it could fill out its images of the human. A sensitivity to the science, poetry, philosophy, art and religion of today would reestablish our bonds with the non-human universe and re-establish man as shepherd of creation who gently clears a space in the wilderness that all things may be. Underneath his veneer of rational control man "craves that empathy clinging between man and beast, that nagging shadow of remembrance which, try as we may to deny it, asserts our unity and does more. Paradoxically, it establishes, in the end, our own humanity. One does not meet oneself until one catches the reflection from an eye other than human."[10]

In the stage of ecumenical religion/Christianity the final norm of truth is human experience. In earlier times this statement would have been taken to exclude revelation. But Julian Huxley's religion without revelation was no better than religions that possessed a revelation. What was needed was a framework of experience large enough to include both the revelational and

9. Constantinos Doxiadis, *The New World of Urban Man* (Philadelphia, 1965), p. 34.
10. Loren Eiseley, *The Unexpected Universe* (New York, 1969), p. 24.

the religious. Experience should not be equated to what is empirically evident and scientifically measurable. In fact, it is not clear just what is contained in experience but it is certain that experience goes beyond what any one man can embrace. Experience is less what a man has than what a man addresses and what mankind is addressed by.

The taking of experience as the norm of truth has been dangerous in the past because there has always been one group who decided where experience stops. They were the same ones who set themselves up to be interpreters of other people's experience. Such a power relationship inevitably slides from an interpreting of experience to substituting for it. The norm of truth then becomes not the experience as interpreted by doctrine but the doctrine which dictates to experience. Within the walls of church educational institutions this reversal has almost always happened. Fortunately, American Christian theology has often done better than that when it dealt with social issues. "For American theology and ethics, norms come proximately from communal experience in reorganizing space through a form of feedback rather than from authority, whether biblical or traditionary. There may be a place for biblical norms and the norms of ecclesiastical tradition, but this place is validated through a contest with experience, and ultimately through the consent of experience rather than through the ontological persistence of the original authority."[11]

People who demand that there be a higher norm of truth than human experience are asking for an idol. Man has no recourse in his life except to turn to what is finite. He can submit, as he is always tempted to submit, to a text or a ruler or an institution built by his own hands. There is no lack of things available and waiting for divinization. His only other alternative is to follow his own human experience and to pursue it wherever it takes him. If there be a God, must not his voice be heard within the experience of a man who listens with all other

11. James Sellers, *Public Ethics* (New York, 1970), p. 266.

45

men for the voice of the divine? And as a man does that, might he not discover that none of the things around him is god but that everything he experiences calls him to some great, unexpected mystery? There is something more to his experience than *what* he experiences, some element that is unmistakably there but can never be put into direct focus. "The ultimate or unconditioned element in experience is not so much the seen but the basis of seeing; not what is known as an object so much as the basis of knowing; not an object of value, but the ground of valuing; not the thing before us, but the source of things; not the particular meanings that generate our life in the world, but the ultimate context within which these meanings necessarily subsist."[12]

There has been a theological presumption that Christianity has a direct route to God which short-circuits this plodding path of human experience. This presumption has been the bane of religious education in the churches. It remains so to this day despite all the talk about experience in the religious education field. Leaders of the religious education movement in Protestantism during the early part of this century were keenly aware of this theological issue.[13] It was not that they were replacing faith in God with experience of the social. They were as interested in God as any of their bible toting or neo-orthodox opponents. They simply maintained that the only way to have a more profound faith in God was to deepen awareness of human relationships. Their difference was not on whether God was to be apprehended but *how*. Their question was whether God was to be met through insertion into life or whether God was always to be the point toward which the whole human community strives.[14]

The questions of "what is the purpose of life," "why must

12. Langdon Gilkey, *Naming the Whirlwind* (New York, 1969), p. 296.

13. See: Coe, *op. cit.*, pp. 268–272; Elliot, *op. cit.*, p. 267.

14. See: Robert Johann, *The Pragmatic Meaning of God* (Milwaukee, 1966), p. 57.

I die," "who am I," etc., are still questions which are raised or should be raised within human experience. To these questions Christianity and other religions deeply rooted in human soil should address themselves. There is an unfortunate tendency today to oppose experience to history and to choose the former as preferable. Attempts must be made from several directions to show that experience subsumes history within itself. In this context religion ought to be a force for reminding men of their roots.[15]

Christianity is now engaged in a test of nerve as to whether it can so love the past that it will transform the whole, whether it can speak from the stability and truth of its own tradition in terms which invite a response from differing traditions, whether it can accept the everyday world which is the only one available while joining hands with every positive force that enlarges the world. It is by no means an easy calling given the arrogant façade of much of its own past and the stubborn forces of today that are destroying mankind. But the picture is not hopeless because there are elements in experience which have refused to disappear. Men have banished night from consciousness but they have not succeeded in doing away with it. There is still a search for light and still a struggle in all kinds of symbolic shapes for an immortality. "Now, as always, the workaday world can be transcended in poetry and the other arts. In the shattering emotion of love, beyond the delusions of sensuality, men continue to find entrance to the still point of the turning world. Now as always, the experience of death as man's destiny, if accepted with an open mind and unarmored heart, acquaints us with a dimension of existence which fosters a detachment from the immediate aims of practical life. Now, as always, the philosophical mind will react with awe to the mystery of being revealed in a grain of matter or a human face."[16]

In a context which is ecumenical in this broadest possible

15. See: René Dubos, *So Human An Animal* (New York, 1968), p. 113.
16. Josef Pieper, *In Tune with the World* (New York, 1965), pp. 63 f.

sense, religion has a place and a role to play. Religion emerges at least as strong as it ever was in the past. Christianity also has a place if it is willing to take the humble role of cooperating in the interpretation of human experience.

3. An Educational Anthropology

A FRAMEWORK for ecumenical education requires an understanding of both the theological and educational changes occurring today. The previous chapter has suggested the extent to which the categories of religion are in transition. This chapter will try to point out the crucial change taking place at the center of educational theory. The picture can only be sketched but there may be a certain virtue in getting the main outline clear rather than going into all the details. Many attempts in religious education to bring together education and religion move quickly past the premises and into the details of the program. Thus, it is presumed that the contribution of the educational theorist is to describe the development of the child to which can be matched a sequence of bible stories and Christian Doctrine. Most of the deficiency in this procedure comes from the theological side but there is also a failure here from the educational point of view. The failure results from assuming that the educational contribution is almost solely a matter of developmental psychology. No one can deny that psychology has made a great contribution to the improvement of education and that other great contributions are still to come. Nevertheless, psychology at the service of education has to be set within the framework of other human questions that are posed by philosophy and the social sciences.

In the latter part of the nineteenth century psychological studies were begun that brought about an overhaul in the educational methods being used in the schools. For the first time, the learning process was scientifically investigated and the gross inefficiency of the school-teacher's work could be reduced. It was John Dewey's greatness to be able to perceive the far reaching implications of educational change. He raised the questions to the explicitly philosophical and socio-political level. From that point onward, progress in education was mainly to come from discussions that were more concerned with anthropology rather than psychology, experience rather than knowledge, and the social rather than the individualistic. In making this statement, of course, one must beware of opposing these words instead of understanding that the first word of each set subsumes the second.

We have already seen the centrality of anthropology, experience and social change to theology. In a movement which preceded theology's and parallels it today, education is also centered on these categories. I have tried to show in regard to theology that this orientation is not the result of a small clique of theologians who are subverting the faith of our fathers, but that the anthropological, social and experiential characteristics of Christianity are intrinsic to it and have always been at least implicit in its presentation. In similar fashion, the directions of American education are not traceable to the idiosyncrasies of John Dewey or the ideology of any small group. Lawrence Cremin, in his *Transformation of the School,* has traced modern American education to its roots in the nineteenth century. Progressive education began as part and parcel of that broader program of social and political reform called the Progressive Movement. Contrary to the widespread conception that it dates from the advent of the Progressive Education Association in 1919, the idea had its origins during the quarter century before World War I in an effort to cast the school as a fundamental lever of social and political regeneration. It began as a many-sided protest against a restricted view of the school, but it was always more than this, for essentially it viewed education as an adjunct to politics in realizing the promise of American life."[1]

1. Lawrence Cremin, *The Transformation of the School* (New York, 1961), p. 88.

In trying to develop an anthropology for education it is important to keep this social context in view. A complete anthropology would be one that is concerned with all of the social relationships that structure human life. When the "social dimension" is brought into educational discussions it is often assumed that one teaches the individual about social problems so that he can go out and change the world. But this procedure simply trivializes the social and frustrates the individual. To take account of the social it is necessary to understand the individual as always set within a social framework that is at once his lifeblood and his constriction. The social structure is not what one talks about in school; it is the reality within which the schooling happens.[2]

A related failure in educational writing is to assume that in the final analysis the question of education is the relating of the teacher to the student. One can hardly overestimate the importance of the personal relationship between teacher and student. The writing in religious education throughout the last few decades has rightfully dwelt on this theme. Nevertheless, it must still be insisted upon that American education includes many other questions than the I-thou attitude of teachers. An anthropological understanding that neglects the political, social and economic elements will eventually make personalistic attitudes of teachers more difficult and less effective. In tracing the decline of Progressivism in America, Cremin charges that the leaders lost sight of their own historical roots and narrowed their vision of education. "Bemused by the ancient truism that as the teacher goes, so goes the school, the [Progressive Education] Association neglected the equally important dictum that he who pays the piper calls the tune. In its definition of the movement it so limited its scope as to cut itself off from many of the most progressive elements of the time, and in its persistent fear of radicalism it shunned the arduous business of marshalling the

2. See: Mario Fantini and Gerald Weinstein, *Making Urban Schools Work* (New York, 1968), pp. 18 f.

diverse political forces that might have supported its cause. In the end, the PEA's failure was neither financial nor philosophical, but ultimately political: it simply failed to comprehend the fundamental forces that move American education."[3]

I would maintain that the starting point for an educational anthropology is the question of freedom and social organization. I will take up this issue first. Only then will I try to analyze the human capacities for learning. They are to be understood in relation to changing the social structure for the increase of freedom. Thus, I move from the social to the individual and back to the social. I hope to show why this is the proper sequence to follow in educational theorizing. It is *a fortiori* the pattern to follow in describing the pattern of religious education.

A few years ago in *Catechesis of Revelation* I wrote that the problem in religious education is freedom. I would hesitate to put it that way today. My hesitancy does not spring from the fact that there is less concern today with freedom; quite the contrary is the case. What had seemed to be the faint chant of a few demonstrators has in a few years become the deafening roar of a whole generation. But precisely because of this development I would be hesitant to say that freedom is the central problem in *religious* education. It would be like saying that the concerns of religious educators should be world peace and universal justice. No one could deny that these are valid concerns but it sounds pretentious if not ridiculous to claim that they are particularly one's own. If a group is going to make any contribution to the great issues of peace, justice or freedom, it must begin by seeing these problems not as its problems or the church's problems but as the problems of everyone. The recognition that freedom is a problem much too big for us to handle should not send us back to easier topics and smaller problems. Freedom is indeed the issue and we must address ourselves to it. My point is that we must be aware that our modest contribution can be made only as we relate it to the worldwide struggle for

3. Cremin, *op. cit.,* p. 273.

freedom. Before asking what religious educators can do for freedom, we have to give attention to the contemporary struggles that far transcend church problems of freedom.

The following brief analysis of the problem of freedom is an attempt to describe in the concrete the peculiar problem of our time. I will prescind from many other questions that would have to be dealt with in a full treatment of the subject. As one surveys the daily uprisings reported by the news media, he is struck by the marvelous means of communication now available and at the same time the almost total absence of communication. There is endless talk about this failure to communicate but this talk itself is not communicating much. Contrary to the general impression, the problem is much more severe than that of one side not clearly explaining its case to the other. The more profound problem today is the value of rational discourse itself. Those who have been brought up to believe that reason is the best hope of humanity are among the most uncomprehending spectators on the scene today. Those who trust in reason and orderly change are shocked to find themselves reclassified on the side of those whom they had considered to be the opponents of change. In fact, those who have been working for progress sometimes find themselves accused of being the worst enemies of the people because they entice people with reasonable improvements within an intolerable system. Before dismissing the opponents of reason, the liberal advocate of change ought to take stock of his own premises. He should understand that his answers are being rejected because it is the premises of his system that are in question. In fact, the challenge today is to the presuppositions of every social system. One need not give up one's reason in order to reconsider whether reason is the all sufficient instrument in this situation. The relation of reason to social change must be looked at very carefully.

Despite all the talk about community and social structure, most people's ideas on freedom seem straight out of the rugged individualism of another century. The difference today is that the more aggressive aspects of individualism are covered by a veneer of rationality. One has to be subtle in getting to the top or at least show some courtesy. It is still thought possible to get up to any point on the ladder of success by making the right choices. The amazing thing is that for a large and an increasing number in the society, the belief has a firm basis. The social system that we assume to be the normal one serves most of us quite handsomely.

The trouble with this advancement of the majority is that it is made largely at the expense of the minority. This fact is something that we either do not like to think about or else is something we just cannot believe. We bear no malice toward those who are less fortunate; in fact, we wish them well. How can we possibly be guilty? The answer is that we are part of a social organization which constantly expands possibilities for greater numbers but which consistently narrows the real field of choice for other people. We assume that people would do all right if they would make the right choices. We do not consider the possibility that all the available choices might be wrong ones. When a man is faced with such a situation and is told to be more reasonable about his choices, then the situation is only exacerbated. Within an organization in which one's position relative to the whole society gets progressively worse, patience with one's problems is not much of a solution.

The point that I am making is hardly a new one but it seems impossible for most people to assimilate the fact. With the constant expansion of the national economy it is presumed that everyone is better off. If there are unskilled workers whose plight grows constantly worse, the fault must be theirs; and if there are millions on welfare, it must be because they are too lazy to work. Why do not people use their freedom and change their position in the society? Those who are served well by the organization find it easy to overlook the immense help which the organization supplies to their own exercise of freedom.

Economists and other social theorists have been trying in

recent years to get this problem seen on the panoramic screen of international affairs. This awakening is a still more difficult task than getting consideration on a national level. The statistics of the incredible lopsidedness of the world's goods do not lie.[4] Yet people either cannot believe that there is anything wrong or else they despair of doing anything to right the situation. William Luijpen has written: "It is perfectly clear, of course, that *we* ourselves did not create it, but this alibi does not express what is most important. For we live in and by that situation. I am able to write this book because I belong to the seventeen per cent who have eighty per cent of the world's wealth at their disposal. Others, like me, plan international congresses, build theatres and churches, promote longer vacations and better educational systems. But all this we can do because we belong to the seventeen per cent. Whatever we gratefully receive from our culture and civilization is stained by an objective sinfulness, from which no sacramental absolution can absolve us. On the other hand, it is also impossible to 'withdraw our hands' and stay idle in order not to soil them. He who withdraws his hands makes them dirty, for he commits a sin of omission; he leaves everything as it is—inhuman. There is but one way out, and that is reform on a worldwide scale."[5]

The problem of freedom, therefore, is not so much one of convincing people to make the right choices but of changing social organization to the extent that right choices are available for all. If enough people do not soon come to understand this fact and work together for basic changes, then another group who do not understand will do the changing. This latter group will be those who find existing social forms intolerable and will change them by destroying the society. A few years ago such a prophecy would have been dismissed as fanciful, but there is

4. For example, see Paul Ehrlich and Anne Ehrlich, *Population, Resources and Environment* (New York, 1970).

5. William Luijpen, *Phenomenology and Atheism* (Pittsburgh, 1964), p. 160.

now accumulated evidence of what may lie in store for us. The more complicated the structure is and the more dependent it is on technology, the fewer are the number of people who would be needed to paralyze a society. If only for its own self-survival, no society can disregard its discontented minorities who are not part of the main march in the quest for freedom.

What we need is an adequate social apparatus, that is, one which makes use of human resources in a way that is proportionate to the needs of all human beings. What we usually have is an inadequate organization that is left over from another century. The elements of the system may have been adequate for another day but they are now obstacles to human growth in freedom. The most tragic aspect of the story is not that we are burdened with archaic institutions but that we get used to them and do not realize how hopelessly outdated they are. As a matter of fact, the things which are the greatest obstacles to freedom are often cited as wonderful instruments of progress. Let me give one glaring example: the automobile. At the turn of the century the automobile looked like an advance and it could have been a step at that time toward something better. Today, despite all the evidence staring us in the face that the automobile has been a disaster, it is still hailed as a marvelous invention that increases the power and freedom of the human race. Instead of everyone working feverishly to change the entire system of mass transportation in our cities and between our cities, we cover the countryside with ugly concrete that worsens the problem. Who suffers most from this inhuman organization? The poor in our cities who have no powerful lobby to get them an adequate transportation system. Those who have money demand and get greater speed, diversity and convenience while the poor still cannot get to a job, to a hospital or to stores that do not over-charge them. Compared to what is both humanly necessary and technologically possible, the transportation in our cities is ludicrous and scandalous. There is no freedom without communication. If the social system makes it continually more difficult to communicate with others, then the principles on which the whole system operates must be drastically changed. A society that fails to transport its people in ways that are both possible and necessary will eventually come to a standstill, that is, it will die. Unless we get a coalition of men with vision, technique, courage and compassion to overcome the coalition that controls transportation in the country, then the powerful interests that are now destroying the poor in our society will eventually destroy us all.

The conclusion I have drawn to my example should be carefully noted. If the system is systematically destroying some people it is destroying all of us. The diminishing of any man's freedom is an attack upon my own. We are all responsible for all, whether or not we face up to the responsibility. It is more obvious than ever that all problems and all peoples are interconnected and that an uprising or revolution in one part of the system will have reverberations in everyone's life. There is a more subtle and more dangerous attack, however, that an inadequate social system launches against each man's freedom.

If a system caters to a certain kind of rational choice, not only are some people denied a place in the system but also a certain part of my own psyche must be submerged or denied. Inadequately developed organization eliminates some people totally but it eliminates all people at least partially. For example, a system that tries to do away with disorderly people is attacking the disorderly part of myself. The system can eventually produce people who really believe that all trouble is caused by a conspiratorial other; the system has cut them off from the troublesome part of themselves. Spontaneity, emotion or any unusual trait appears as a threat because it calls up memory of a part of oneself that was supposed to have been eliminated. Philip Slater writes: "Radical challenges to our society, then, always tap a confused responsive chord within us that is far more disturbing than anything going on outside. They threaten to reconnect us with each other, with nature, and with ourselves, a possibility that is thrilling but terrifying—as if we had grown a shell-like epidermis and someone was threatening to rip it off."[6]

It would follow that an important measure of the freedom of each individual is whether the society protects the rights of some individuals to be different from the standards considered normal. There are individuals whom Erickson describes as "loyal rebels who refuse to adjust to 'conditions' and cultivate indignation in the service of a to-be-restored wholeness."[7] Society starves for differences that are manifest in the lives of artists, mystics or rebellious heroes. However, it is willing to accept these differences only in ways that are safe and nonthreatening. A society is always ambivalent towards its own prophets and saviors. Society almost invariably gets more than the rulers of the society can bear. Some of the prophetic individuals must be sacrificed in order that the status quo can be maintained. Referring to Socrates' death, Hegel wrote that "it was a force within themselves that they were punishing." Those like Socrates who are in contact with some *daimonic* force below the surface of everyday conformity are indeed a threat because they herald the death of an old order and they threaten the personal identity of each man in that order.[8] It is frightening, almost beyond endurance, to discover that the world one had identified as one's own is the tip of a volcano. The conscious and rational world is but a "strategic and not always representative sampling" of one's many unconscious worlds.[9]

The more inadequate the social system becomes the more rational it is likely to be and the more praised is its rationality. While the system is cutting off human life at its roots, this

6. Philip Slater, *The Pursuit of Loneliness* (Boston, 1970), p. 26; see also Erich Neumann, *Depth Psychology and a New Ethic* (New York, 1969), p. 95.

7. Erik Erikson, *Insight and Responsibility* (New York, 1964), p. 156.

8. See Rollo May, *Love and Will* (New York, 1969), pp. 146–150; R. D. Laing *The Politics of Experience* (New York, 1967), p. 141.

9. Richard Jones, *Feeling and Fantasy in Education* (New York, 1968), p. 60.

excising is hailed as a liberating process. Freedom becomes identified with rationality even though rationality may be functioning as an obstacle to freedom. In the name of order in the system all kinds of human experiences are ruthlessly denied. A whole underside of nonrational forces seethes ominously below the surface. For the most part, the guardians of order in the system try to pretend that such a force is not there. When its existence is too evident not to deny, then it is by definition excluded from what is human.

When a society has arrived at the point where men must choose between the rational and the irrational, that society is in proximate danger of destruction. To choose either is to choose against the human and yet these two may seem to be the only alternatives. "The tendency to distrust reason as such in our culture has arisen from the fact that the alternatives presented to intelligent and sensitive people have seemed to be only arid rationalism on the one hand, in which one saves one's mind by losing one's soul or vitalistic romanticism on the other, in which there has seemed at least a chance of saving one's soul for the time being."[10]

Those who decide to save their souls for the time being are genuinely in touch with something real. They have behind them and gushing through them the life force of a million years. Once unleashed these irrational forces can bring down any rational empire. The people who do the unleashing are likely to be exultant because their force has proved superior in battle. "Some artists, some poets, some 'hysterical' people who rely heavily on feeling, emotion, intuition, and impulsiveness, some religious people, the more mystical people are apt to stop right there. They may then repudiate knowledge, education, science, and intellect as destroyers of instinctive feeling, of innate intuition, of natural piety, of innocent perspicuity. I think this strain of anti-intellec-

10. Rollo May, *Existential Psychology* (New York, 1961), p. 49.

tual suspicion runs far deeper than we realize, even in intellectuals themselves."[11]

The negation of the rational has certain apparent virtues to it. There is an end to hypocrisy, insincerity and dishonesty, vices which are the products of a distinctively rational nature. The nonrational life has a forcefulness and directness to it which supplies the individual with a daily dose of joy and/or sadness, feelings which he tends to lose within the confines of human institutions. But this strength is also a danger and what emerges from the irrational is a mirror image of the rational world that is negated. After reason is pushed aside, writes Kenneth Keniston, "what is left is of course instinct, passion and feeling. Yet, separated from reason, these potentially benign and liberating forces have been more and more reduced to blind animal drives. In an individual, when the basic instincts are separated from controlling intelligence, they tend to become crude and bestial; and so, in intellectual history, the cleavage between the apostles of passion and the advocates of mind has brought an abasement of our conception of passion to an equation with the forces of destructiveness, self-seeking, the call of the blood, and the imperatives of lust."[12]

Just as the nonrational force cannot be entirely banished in the rational stronghold, so neither does reason entirely disappear in an age when indiscriminate passion is let loose. The rational plays its part but in slightly corrupted form; it appears in the simplistic but powerful combination of ideas called an ideology. "Images of the world involving truths which are obvious to all do not become ideologies. It is the half truth, or at least the insecure truth, which appeals to some but not to others, which is the best candidate to set up an ideology."[13] A few years ago there was proclamation of the "end of ideology," a pronounce-

11. Abraham Maslow, *The Psychology of Science* (New York, 1966), p. 63.
12. Kenneth Keniston, *The Uncommitted* (New York, 1965), p. 329.
13. Kenneth Boulding, *The Meaning of the Twentieth Century* (New York, 1964), p. 164.

ment that was true only in a very restricted way. Ideologies which are total explanations of the universe have fallen on bad times and perhaps will never recover. But the passing of more systematic ideologies only opens the door to more fleeting and volatile ideologies. In Robert Lifton's description of what he calls the "protean man" of today, he writes: "One also encounters in protean man what I would call strong ideological hunger. He is starved for ideas and feelings that can give coherence to his world, but here too his taste is toward new combinations. While he is by no means without yearning for the absolute, what he finds most acceptable are images of a more fragmentary nature than those of the ideologies of the past; and these images, although limited and often fleeting, can have great influence upon his psychological life. Thus political and religious movements, as they confront protean man, are likely to experience less difficulty convincing him to alter previous convictions than they do providing him a set of beliefs which can command his allegiance for more than a brief experimental attitude."[14]

If the choice of either alternative, rationality or irrationality, leads to disaster, where do we go from here? The answer which comes almost too quickly to one's lips is wholeness, integrity or the total man. The reason for my saying that the answer is too obvious and too quickly stated is because those who give glib answers about dealing with the whole man often have not even begun to grasp what the problem is. They do not understand why the problem originally arises nor do they comprehend the difficulty of reaching a point where one can indeed deal with the whole.

In regard to the unity of man there are not two positions, integralist and fragmentarian. Everyone who uses an educational anthropology claims to have an integral, unified picture of man.

14. Robert Lifton, *History and Human Survival* (New York, 1970), p. 324.

In some sense, every one does have a picture of the whole man but there are three quite different ways of arriving at unity.

In the first place there is a way of getting unity by not introducing distinctions. In practice it is more often a blurring of distinctions. Education books have often spun out a hazy rhetoric of concern for the whole person, but with little clarification of what this means. The distinctions, of course, do creep in because whole people are not wholly available in any direct way. This unavoidable fact of life gives rise to the second kind of integrity or unity.

The second approach to unity works by simply combining the pieces. The problem of human unity is here understood to be the mechanical one of weighing equal amounts. A balance of rationality and nonrationality, intelligence and freedom, understanding and action is advocated. For example, some writers in education have rediscovered the emotional. It is presumed by them that education has neglected this side of man and, just as obviously, that there should now be emphasis on this side. They are attacking a real ill but the cure promises to be worse than the disease. It is inaccurate to say that education is too rational. Schools are very rational in some ways but very irrational in other ways. Schools have never neglected the affective part of life; they have sometimes subtly manipulated the emotional and at other times openly exploited it. The trouble is the *separation* of the rational and nonrational. Separation is never overcome by pressing the two parts together; some more primordial kind of unity has to be found. The concentration on the nonrational in order to balance the picture is a dangerous move, particularly when made by people who think that it is an easy job to straighten out human beings by adding a few correctives. If behavior is poor, or education does not change behavior to their liking, then the presumed solution is to add courses on behavioral change or add techniques that will change behavior. If the curriculum is called irrelevant, then the solution is thought to be to add some "relevant" material to the curriculum.

It is difficult to oppose the proponents of this position because what they are mostly doing is restating the question, although their restatements are less helpful than the original questions.

The third approach to the whole man is one which has a difficult time getting a hearing. The advocates of the other kinds dismiss it as unnecessarily complex or lacking in unity. This position tries to find a comprehensive framework which will bear some distinctions. From a primitive kind of unity, it proceeds to distinction with instruments of analysis, in order to come back to a deeper but *still tentative* unity. It sees that the problem of human unity is not met by mouthing a formula but by understanding how man is a unity. For example, thinking and feeling can be distinguished; they should not be separated but they can be distinguished for the purpose of interrelating them within a unity. Likewise, understanding and behavior are distinguishable; the question is not whether to distinguish them but how to relate them. If one were to reject the words I have just used he would still have to use some categories for distinguishable human elements so that there can be progress in understanding the human and living humanly.

The first position leads to an unintended separation; the second position assumes a separation. The third position recognizes that separation is the enemy of unity. Thus, the third position begins and ends with unity while allowing the full play of rational categories in between. Schools have failed not by concentrating too much on the mind but by separating the mind from the larger context. It is the split itself which must be overcome or else we are doomed to rationalism and sentimentality, often living inside the same person.

A more viable approach to the question of unity is to begin with categories that are comprehensive and also can be clarified by distinctions. The choice of words has some arbitrariness to it but there must be some continuity with the past and a high degree of consistency in their present use. I use the word experience to designate the totality of human interaction with the environment. I use the word understanding for the assimilation of that experience in a specifically human way. Finally, I use the word intelligence to designate the ability to deal with experience in a way that leads to understanding. Experience includes, therefore, both rational and nonrational elements. Likewise, understanding includes within itself thinking and feeling. In this use of terms intelligence is wider than reason because it subsumes the nonrational as well. In the following few pages I would like to suggest what this choice of words means.

The word experience is the key anthropological word here.[15] At least in the American language it is the word that has provided direction for philosophical, psychological, social and political theory. Largely through Dewey, though not exclusively through him, it has dominated educational discussion in America. Unfortunately, in this last context its meaning has been trivialized. Experience has been taken to mean the things which the students have had which are the jumping off point for where the teacher wishes to go. This use of the word neglects all the rich connotations of experience and fails to comprehend the dramatic change which this category should introduce.

The word experience is significant in American development because it immediately connotes the relational. A word like knowledge is less helpful as a starting point because of historical problems connected with it, that is, knowledge has too often functioned as the data which a subject possesses about an objective world. If one begins with such a dichotomy there is no way to get a relational (personal, social, political) world as a conclusion. Experience is the fundamental mode of being that undercuts a split between subject and object. Experience has a subjective pole and an objective pole but they are distinguishable within the comprehension of experience.

As one aspect of this relational character, experience is a practical mode of being; it comprehends theory and practice. A person does not so much have experience as participate with

15. See: Fontinell, *op. cit.,* pp. 52–61.

others in experience. It is what the humans are always engaged in.

The understanding or misunderstanding of the category of experience gives rise to two different educational anthropologies. These two are conflicting anthropologies even though they may use the same words. The first will try to locate thinking elements within experience that would modify behavior in a way not entirely predictable. The second will seek to get a person to think (or feel) in a way that will make his behavior conform to some standard. The first is social and practical even when it uses an abstract language. It begins with man as an acting and receiving organism. Its question is not what to run into the switchboard but which plugs to pull in a board that is always flooded with messages. The second anthropology is individualistic and abstract even when it talks about the social and aims at feelings. It works too hard at giving the person the right experience, right ideas and right action. This anthropology talks about experience but trivializes it, cultivates emotion but distorts it, aims at behavior but aborts it.

It seems to be a tragic fact of life that schools and teachers, despite good intentions, inevitably fall back into this second anthropology. The main reason, I would suggest, is that the hardening of two categories, school and teacher, necessarily results in the second anthropology. In explaining this point I will be elaborating and exemplifying the relational and practical character of experience.

The first anthropology, in order to be sustained in education, would require constant interaction of teacher and learner to a degree precluded by nearly all schools of today. The test of this interaction would be whether the roles of teacher and learner interchange. Experience is not what the student comes with nor is it what the teacher supplies but it is what teacher and student take part in. As they participate within it and try to illuminate it, each is teacher toward the other as is also each a learner toward the other. If the teacher has not learned while teaching, he has not taught; and if the learner has not taught while learning he has not learned. They do not necessarily have to participate *equally* in both roles. The one who gets paid for the job of teaching and is usually older should presumably have the role of teacher for more than fifty per cent of the time. However, even those two criteria will not be enough to distinguish teachers in the future since students will also get paid for learning and may be as old as the teachers. The distinguishing mark of the one who has the main teacher role is that he should have more knowledge or specialized skills. But if he totally identifies with the role and never learns with and from those he is teaching, he has lost contact with experience. Anyone who teaches six-year-olds or sixteen-year-olds and finds nothing to learn from them has indeed lost contact.

The inability of the teacher to learn is not entirely his fault. The system to a large extent puts the wrong learners in school and separates school from life. There ought to be a school and a nonschool pole within experience. Like teacher/student there is a place for a definite structure. It should be fairly clear what is a school and what is not a school but the two should not be so rigid that they never interchange. Schools veer wildly from trying to be an "experience of life itself" to being ghettos unconnected with life. Within the experience of life the school and nonschool elements should be distinguished but also related in such a way that one is constantly modifying the other.

I shall return in the next chapter to these relationships within education. My point here is simply to show that if one takes the practical, relational category of experience as primary, then one can proceed to some distinctions within that category that will illuminate experience. No one knows fully what may be included in his own experience because it is not fully or exclusively his. In therapy, in education and in life itself the main job is to see what is there, accept that as oneself and find ways to direct it gently toward greater wholeness.

Both Maslow and Rogers describe therapy as the removing

of obstacles to a fuller experience of oneself.[16] The patient probably comes in order to solve some problems or get rid of some wrong behavior. He is on the way to being cured when he stops trying to cure his problems and begins to experience himself, that is, he lets be aspects of experience that up to now he would not admit existed. Reason is not overthrown but its function is changed from that of dictating what may exist to that of serving experience by discriminating and illuminating it.

The most comprehensive term for this assimilation of experience is understanding. The correlative of understanding is intelligence; a man is intelligent to the degree that he can understand. In this sense intelligence is a practical, relational and receptive capacity. This use of the word is at considerable variance with the way the word has come to be used in academic circles. It is closely akin, however, to John Holt's definition of intelligence as "how we behave when we don't know what to do."[17] By this standard many professors are not very intelligent though they may be highly rational. Likewise, some ghetto children, who have low I.Q.'s but have learned to survive in an urban jungle, may be highly intelligent.

The distinction between intelligence and reason seems to me to be a crucial one that must be maintained despite the constant blurring of terms in their general use. Of course, one might prefer to make the same distinction by using other terms; for example, substantive reason and functional reason. However, the words intelligence, intellect, intelligent and intellectual are worth trying to salvage for this purpose. A contrast of the two words, reason and intelligence, in their relation to freedom might show why I insist on this distinction.

Reason works within a closed system, drawing conclusions from established premises. It leads to choice among given alternatives. Reason is an inestimable good but it is valuable only at the service of life. If it tries to dictate to life by closing off new

16. See: Rogers, *op. cit.*, p. 80; Maslow, *op. cit.*, p. 54.
17. John Holt, *How Children Fail* (New York, 1964), p. 165.

experience, then it is a great danger to life and in trying to suppress life it will destroy itself. For most of us whose lives are quite stable and well fixed in the established order, we almost invariably make of freedom a rational thing. Those who oppose this assumption (in our vocabulary they are sometimes called "culturally deprived") are warning us that the identification of freedom and reason may not lead to a very bad life but it certainly will not lead to a very good life. More importantly they are warning us that though reason may seem to work for a long while, the irrational will explode and reassert itself. Particularly in days like our own when the times have become unhinged, there is a call for practical men who embody reasonable answers from the past. This is a temptation to which we must not succumb. We need visionary men who understand life deeply enough to break the rules of reason in order to create a new social pattern in which men can get on with life.

The quest for freedom is the resurgence of intelligence above reason. Intelligence is man's capacity to deal with life as a whole. It includes within itself the entire spectrum of human affectivity. Although feeling may not include intelligence, intelligence always subsumes feeling within itself. An intelligent man cannot but be a passionate man. Intelligence not only sees life as it is but as it can be. It is man's possibility of thinking through a fundamental reorientation of social patterns, not so much by choosing from among alternatives as by creating new alternatives. The aim of intelligence is to understand life rather than oppose it, not to suppress spontaneity but to enlarge it. The intelligent man is the one who can accept into his life more than he can rationally manipulate. He does not deny what he cannot immediately grasp; he is able to suspend judgment. In this regard, one of the tests of both freedom and intelligence is the ability to relinquish at times the conscious control of life and face without fear the impulses arising from more primitive layers of personality.

This use of the word intelligence would enable us to say that a school should always be an intelligent place. It would give us some hints of what an intelligent place would be like. It would also get rid of the dangerous and absurd charge that schools are overly concerned with intelligence and that teaching is too intellectual. In my use of the word, it is simply impossible to be too intellectual, that is, too interested in persons perceiving, symbolizing, understanding and directing experience.

What is meant by the charge that education is too intellectual is that it is too rational. This claim could be true but I suspect that it is usually not. Where reason has become deified and has constructed systems of speculation unchecked by experience, then education is indeed too rational. Actually, where an excess of rationality is charged, reason may be hardly operating at all. One should not dignify with the word reason the boring recital of useless information. Alfred North Whitehead once wrote that "fatigue is the antithesis of Reason. The operations of fatigue constitute the defeat of reason in its primitive character of reaching after the upward trend. Fatigue means the operation of excluding the impulse toward novelty."[18] I would submit that very few educational institutions anywhere exhibit an excess of reason, but that a great many of them are afflicted with reason's enemy, fatigue.

I would like to put together this anthropological description in a three step pattern not unlike the three phases described in the preceding chapter. The similarity of the two schema is not entirely accidental. In Chapter 2, I distinguished primitive religion, narrow Christianity and ecumenical religion/Christianity. These three are not necessarily steps in a sequence but they do indicate possible phases of growth for a society and for individuals. In a parallel manner, I have described in this chapter three levels of experience. The first is a primitive kind of involvement in action. The human being is born into a social matrix of experience which is there from before the time he is conscious. This first level is most obviously described as feeling, that is, a

18. A. N. Whitehead, *The Function of Reason* (Boston, 1958), p. 23.

direct, unreflective, sensed encounter with the world. It could also be referred to as primitive intellect in the less obvious sense that the organism absorbs the world in a vast range of practical, symbolic activities.

A second level of experience is that of reason in which the subjective power of control arises. The world is not just met but analyzed and dictated to. Man becomes keenly aware of his identity by self-reflectively differentiating himself from the objects about him. Reason is of its nature selective and controlling. Man has survived at all only because he could name the animals and because he could decide what to be attentive to in his experience. Reason is such a great gift that it can act as a seductress, no longer as gift to life but as better than life. Ideas can become a substitute for action and experience can become mechanically excluded from the conscious world. These processes, if they go on unchecked, corrupt themselves and produce an abstract and dehumanized world.

There is a third level of experience which is intellectual understanding. This stage picks up some of the valuable elements from the first stage which reason tends to forget. Reason is not left behind but it is given a healthier context in which to operate, that is, the modes of interaction that precede reason and are closer to life. A scientific explanation from man's reason is in most respects superior to a mythical story of primitive intellect, but there is a higher form of understanding which can incorporate both of them. Likewise, there is a passivity which is sub-rational in which there is simply absorption. There is secondly an activity of reason which is a striving for mastery. There is finally an attitude which is actively passive or passively active in which one is supremely intent on doing nothing but receiving. In trying to understand someone, Maslow writes, one must get his brain out of the way.[19] He must let his reason rest and exercise his intelligence.

This attitude of receptivity is not a return to the primitive,

19. Maslow, *op. cit.,* pp. 10 f., 96.

awe-struck and fear-ridden attitude that precedes reason. It is, on the contrary, a transcending of reason which is possible only by discipline and communion. It is an attitude which carries a joy in understanding even in the midst of sorrows. Toward such understanding all education should move and to such education an ecumenical study could make a powerful contribution.

4. An Ecumenical Framework

IN the previous two chapters I have outlined a pattern of religious development and a picture of man in education. The step to be taken in this chapter is the marriage of these two schema in order to produce an ecumenical framework for education. The two chapters that follow this one will fill out this framework with more concrete material pertaining to the three stages of development.

Before considering any kind of curriculum for formal education, it is necessary to reflect upon the aims of education and the components of the educational process. Religious education has been a hazy venture partly because the notion of education itself is not entirely clear. The word education is exposed, on the one hand, to becoming so generalized that it is in danger of losing its meaning; or, on the other hand, it can be so narrowly conceived that it loses its life-giving relationships to the rest of existence. Both pitfalls must be avoided.

As I have pointed out in the preceding chapter, education, at least in the American tradition, has been an adjunct of political and social change. From the time of Thomas Jefferson's warning that "if a nation expects to be ignorant and free in a state of civilization, it expects what never was and never will be," there has nearly always been a close relationship between education and the social order and between knowledge and political freedom.

There have always been others, of course, who claim that education ought to concentrate on the individual and that education ought to produce men who can stand against the crowd.[1]

1. See John Stoops, *Religious Values in Education* (Danville, Ill., 1967).

This objection is usually not to the point since it presumes that the alternatives are either social or individualistic, conformity or autonomy. With these as alternatives, some people can write stirring rhetoric in favor of individual freedom but such sentiments have little reference to the actual environment in which men live. The real task in education is to comprehend the social and the individual in a way that does violence to neither. I have claimed that if one begins with the social and proceeds to the individual, one has a much better chance of correct analysis than if one begins with the individual and tries to get at the social order. Thus, education's allegiance with social and political change not only does not neglect the individual but calls forth the individual's powers in the most effective context. It is the job of education to confront social problems with intelligence and through the use of intelligence to strive for an order in which the goals of both the self and others are included.

An educational approach that attempts to fix on the individual without taking seriously the social structuring of his life will inevitably tend to oppose change. An unchanging essence of man is held up as the ideal, and at the same time fixed procedures for instructing the individual are employed to reach this ideal. During much of history such education has had the value of giving a certain stability to people and of providing the feeling that they had control over their lives. Throughout the last century and particularly in the last few decades, such education has had greater and greater difficulty in achieving these limited objectives. Change is too all pervasive to dismiss it as peripheral to man and the social order has become too massively visible to be surmounted by individual will power. In our era, the individual is more pressured than ever before to face the relationships and the change that structure his life. He can, of course, withdraw still further into his shell but only with dire consequences. "Only by dying can an American escape the drive for movement and change; this leaves only two alternatives for one who would live as a member of this new social system:

73

either he can be carried along as a passive passenger, or he can be himself a moving force in determining his own destiny. The difference will be in the degree to which he *knows* what the system is."[2]

The individual thus lives in some tension with the social order of which he is a part. Education that is concerned with the social should not be conceived as a process of adjustment for the sake of homeostasis. At the center of education is knowledge, that is, the power of having ideas which can change the world. Much recent discussion of education has revolved around the question of whether education should be primarily concerned with knowledge. This statement of the issue is misleading and dangerous. Education is always concerned with knowledge; any analysis of education must have knowledge to the forefront of the discussion. But there are different kinds of knowledge and different ways of getting knowledge. The deeper issue, therefore, is the relation of knowledge to both experience and freedom.

When Dewey defined education as "that reconstruction or reorganization of experience which adds to the meaning of experience, and which increases ability to direct the course of subsequent experience,"[3] he provided a clue to the kind of knowledge necessary. It is a knowledge that is constructed out of experience and which because it provides a pattern of meaning gives a man greater self-determination. Such knowledge implies a continuity of thinking and feeling, knowledge and freedom, understanding and action. "The construction of knowledge, as distinct from the attainment of it, presumes freedom and skill in the use of controlled emotion and imagery."[4] If this element of discovery or construction is not present at all, it is doubtful that what is happening can be called education. Mental processes which are trained to act through external pressures produce behavior that

2. Solon Kimball and James McClellan, *Education and the New America* (New York, 1962), p. 258.
3. John Dewey, *Experience and Education* (New York, 1938), p. 89.
4. Jones, *op. cit.,* p. 26.

defends against experience rather than copes with it.[5] The supposed knowledge can thus be a block to experience and an obstacle to education. On the other hand, where "knowledge is instrumental to the enrichment of immediate experience through the control over action that it exercises,"[6] there will be creativity and the expansion of human possibilities.

It is possible to speak of education as the chief task of life. By the same token education can be conceived of as a lifelong process. This fact does not mean that every experience of life must be called education. There is a question of quality in experience and the extent to which education is intended and directed. One could draw up some criteria for designating some experiences as educational. For example, wherever there is creative release of power, greater unity of the conscious and unconscious, and more enthusiasm for learning, there is education. My main interest, however, is not in making up an exhaustive list of such criteria. I simply wish to make the point that, although education does consist in a definite set of experiences, it is still valid to extend the word to include a lifelong process.

It must be admitted that educational institutions are not distributed evenly for all ages. It may seem unrealistic to speak of lifelong education when nearly all the institutions exist for children. As a result some people refer to learning as a lifelong process but to education as a task of youth. Nevertheless, it seems preferable to insist today on education being lifelong while admitting that "schooling" is still mainly an affair for the young. This preference for distinguishing education/schooling rather than learning/education reflects a double concern: first, that there should be recognized many other educational instruments operative in our society besides schools. For example, television is or could be a very powerful means of education. Second, although the resources of education are still weighted in

5. See Jerome Bruner, *Toward a Theory of Instruction* (New York, 1966), pp. 146 f.
6. John Dewey, *Art as Experience* (New York, 1958), 290.

the direction of children, the distribution of resources is changing and must change more. Changing the language does not of itself shift institutions but it might help support the growth of an attitude that sees education as a lifelong task.

The ambiguity in this language of education is indicative of a fundamental problem that has recently developed and promises to become worse. Every civilized society has used some form of school to transmit its tradition and re-create itself. When a society is stable and has a body of sacred knowledge to hand over to the young, the role of a school is very clear. As change has accelerated in modern times more and more education was needed and an ever increasing burden of transmission has been put on the school. At the same time, however, this very process of change was undermining the authority that the school had had. As the school kept losing its power to accomplish what it was built for it tried to recoup its losses by extending its activities. As a result, we have the paradox of an ever greater demand for more schools, for a longer school year and for easier admission into schools while at the same time there is widespread criticism and rejection of what goes on in schools particularly by those involved in them.

We are in a terrible bind today which promises to get worse unless the place of the school can be reconsidered. Schools have not only been modified over the past century, they have almost reversed their role. As a stable and conservative institution in the past the school could be a sacred repository for the young. But as more and more weight was placed upon the school it became a place in which the authority of the past is challenged. This reversal was not planned by anyone in particular. It emerged from adaptation to accelerated social change and from correct instincts of what education must become.

Education as lifelong inquiry still requires a formal structure or schooling. But the formal element now is for challenging and critically examining authority. The school would in the long run help to re-establish authority and tradition but only by doing away with all vestiges of authoritarianism from the past. The trouble is that while schools purport to encourage this kind of inquiry, much of the school's structure is itself authoritarian.

The authoritarian image of the school will probably never be erased until schooling becomes a normal element in everyone's life. The paradigm for a school situation should be a learning community in which all of the members participate. But schools confuse the authority of teacher over learner with the authority of adults over children. These two questions have never been distinguished because of the ages of the people in schools. The attempts to reform existing schools do not get at this basic problem. What would seem to be intelligent reforms by sensitive people often make things worse. Although the analogy of students as an oppressed people is faulty, the suppression, exploitation and explosive anger continue to grow.

The problem is not so much the insincerity or authoritarianism of the adults as it is the school structure that now exists. The school works at cross purposes with itself. The proof that school is not really for the transformation of society is that schools are still for children. If schools were places of freedom, inquiry and impetus for social change, they would not be considered places built for children. Schools would be places for everybody some of the time and for no one all of the time. Perhaps there might be years when people would profit from doing almost nothing else except go to school. It would still have to be asked whether those years are not fewer than our society assumes. Furthermore, those years might best be spread throughout life rather than be concentrated in childhood and adolescence. The answers to such questions presuppose that we agree on what a school is and what it should accomplish.

Our world is still trying to live out a decision made at the turn of the century to transform the school into an all encom-

77

passing agent for the youth of the country. "The very conditions that made the school a marginal institution in the agrarian community—its separation from the constantly accelerating changes occurring around it—enabled it to appear as a stable base on which a new comprehensive education could be built."[7] This hope in the schools was probably unrealistic from the start but it is only in recent years that this fact has become apparent. The unrelenting drive toward complexity in society and increase in information now make it realistic to speak of education as being lifelong and life itself. But having given over the job of education to the school in the recent past, American society seems to be sliding toward having school become lifelong and life itself. "Having begun with the belief that education was essential for the formation of a democratic society, we went on to equate the need for education with the demand for school. In the process we have succeeded in transforming the function of the schools from the primary one of education to an emphasis on certifying, sorting and selecting."[8] The society finds, however, that people who have nothing to do for sixteen or twenty years but go to school eventually explode even if it is only out of boredom.

Where we went wrong on this development is fairly easy to grasp and what kind of change would now be needed is also obvious enough. But it would require a realignment of educational resources that at present is beyond the level of feasibility. The school would have to choose the limited function it can perform and re-establish its relation to non-school experience. Perhaps after more small experiments are tried and a few key changes have occurred, the larger system will be able to change in the magnitude urgently needed. "We will actually raise the question whether all those years of sitting in school as a youngster are necessary and useful. We will become impatient at keeping the young in school until they are almost middle-aged,

7. Kimball and McClellan, op. cit., p. 104.
8. Thomas Green, Work Leisure and American Schools (New York, 1968), pp. 153 f.

as is now the fashion. We will, in other words, rediscover experience—but order it on a knowledge basis."[9]

If the schools were the ordering of experience on a knowledge basis, then schools would be freed from the pressure of trying to supply all kinds of experiences which school can only introduce artificially. Schools, on that same basis, would cease to be a preparation for life and would concentrate on whatever life is being experienced, both inside and outside the school. I would point out emphatically that saying school is not a preparation for life is not equivalent to saying that school is life itself. School is not life; it is a small but important part of life in which there is a formal structuring of learning to clarify the experience now available. Progressive sounding statements like "school should be an experience of life" are not contributory to progress at all. They are either too vague to bring about needed change or else they cultivate the already dangerous tendency of schools to intrude into the privacy of individual lives. Furthermore, they may only buttress the assumption that schools are for children and, worse, children are for schools.

Before describing how the school should operate, one must face the prior issue of the relation of school to other educational experience. The very framing of the question in this way could quickly lead to the introduction of freedom into the educational process. As it now is, schools are frustrated in their efforts to be places of freedom because going to school in the first place is not a free act. Children, like everyone else and always to a degree more than adults, necessarily have their freedom defined and limited by the total environment. Nevertheless, there is a degree of freedom and a respect for individual selfhood which cannot be eliminated without suffering irremediably negative consequences. Schools have not succeeded in establishing this level of assuring the dignity of meaningful self-determination. James Coleman has suggested that "one way of opening up the schools would be to have a multitude of components of

9. Peter Drucker, *The Age of Discontinuity* (New York, 1969), p. 323.

79

schools that a boy or girl *could* attend, though no single one was compulsory. Such special purpose 'comprehensive schools' should be, if they are to be successful, the creation of private enterprises through government contracts. The introduction of competition, if the competitors and the students were paid on the basis of production (that is, measured change produced in their students), might bring a wealth of new ways to learn such basic skills as reading and arithmetic efficiently."[10]

This step in the direction of breaking schools into components might lead to a larger change in which some of the components cease to be schools but would still be educational experiences. The school could then function as one point of a triangle of education. The other two points can be called "the laboratory-work context" and "the community seminar context." The nature of these two learning experiences is described by Oliver and Newmann in the following way:

Laboratories are contexts for learning in the midst of action; learning occurs not because it is planned, but only as an inevitable by-product of genuine participation in problem-and-task-oriented activities. The laboratory is seen not as the site of apprenticeship or vocational training for breadwinning, but rather as a place offering the opportunity to satisfy broader humanistic and aesthetic goals. At present many adults are engaged in pursuits in laboratory contexts— mainly their jobs (these are not recognized or supported for their educational value). Young people are deemed not "ready" to participate until they first spend twelve to sixteen years in "school." We believe the laboratory offers important educational benefits at all ages; it should not be restricted to adults.[11]

The major thrust of the seminars is reflection and deliberation, though the questions discussed would be highly relevant to the laboratory context or the world of "action." Learning in the seminar

10. James Coleman, *Adolescents and the Schools* (New York, 1965), p. 104.
11. Fred Newmann and Donald Oliver, "Education and Community," in *Religion and Public Education,* ed. Theodore Sizer, (Boston, 1967), p. 217.

is not preplanned, nor are there specific tasks or problems to solve. Questions are raised, investigated, and discussed; this process, regardless of numerous unpredictable possible outcomes, is of high educational value. Generally both youth and adults are denied the kind of learning afforded by this context—the time of youth is monopolized by school; that of adults, by jobs, or "laboratories."[12]

If these two modes of learning were operative, the school would be left to concentrate upon disciplined activities of the mind. School would be a very intelligent place and also a highly rational place, in the meanings that those two words have been given. The contention that school should be highly rational is not a rationalistic thesis unless one presumes that school is the only means of education there is. While it is true that education deals with the "whole man" in the full range of experience, school ought to restrict itself to challenging the mind with rational tools that will enable the individual to cope with experience. This kind of activity remains necessary for the frail human animal. He must understand how he got to where he is and how to devise means to maintain his precarious balance in the technological and evolutionary world. There will continue to be the need for a place where people can go to find artifacts of human tradition. Books are still the main means available for making contact with the accumulated learning of the past and present. We can hope for rapid expansion of programmed environments that will use not only books but a great variety of machines and materials. There will also still be the need for people who function as teachers in a school. Their job is to devise the environments of learning and be the resources of learning in specialized directions. There may even be a place for the giving of lectures and the correcting of papers provided that people are ready to learn in those ways.

As school now stands a person is subjected to endless hours of it while young. Gradually the time school occupies decreases

12. *Ibid.,* p. 218.

as he gets older. Perhaps it should be the other way around with the least amount of schooling for the child. It is doubtful, in fact, whether a small child needs anything of what I have delineated as school. Possibly the child needs schooling to acquire "basics skills" like reading but even this supposition can be challenged. As George Dennison points out,[13] every child learns to speak in our society without a course training him to talk. Reading is a less difficult skill to learn and in a literate society every child should be able to learn how to read without the school teaching it. Dennison points out with some passion that children in his school did not have a "reading problem" though there were many problems they did have and symptomatic of their problems was the incidental fact that they could not read.

The kind of mini-school that Goodman and Dennison propose[14] (a storefront with 28 children, 4 benevolent adults, and the city about them) fits more into the categories of laboratory and seminar rather than school. The school part of education for children ought to give guidance in learning how to learn, that is, there is a skill to acquiring knowledge and knowing how to use it. Schools ought to be available for providing this help according to individual needs. Such schools, Goodman has written, would not have any drop-outs, only determined drop-ins. The school would provide the helpful elements of guided interaction between teacher and students as also between student and student. Education does not proceed by the continuous absorption of new knowledge but by the constant re-establishment of some unity or model by information that fits or challenges the existing pattern. Since so much of education consists in the challenging of old models with new information, it is important that there be some part of education devoted to the setting out

13. George Dennison, *The Lives of Children* (New York, 1969), p. 190.
14. See Paul Goodman, "Mini-Schools: A Prescription for the Reading Problem," *New York Review of Books*, Jan. 4, 1968.

of a full model of understanding and the challenging of one model by another.[15]

In restricting itself to the role of challenging the mind, the school would decrease in the time it would occupy a person's day. (How many people could bear more than a few ideas each day, if they were really ideas generated by the mind?) But the school enterprise would still be an enormous undertaking of money, people and material. In the long run the school would increase in significance. "Since learning in school would occupy only a small portion of the student's day—perhaps three hours —one might expect the school staff to dwindle. If, however, adults also used the school for instruction, the school's population would increase, even though any given student spent only a small time there. The demand for professional education would remain high."[16]

In this framework schools would be places particularly suited to adults. For a child, the extended and concentrated attention on rational activity inevitably leads to the corruption of intelligence. Their experience cannot sustain that much rational inquiry. As a result, attempts must be made to inject "experiences" into the school or else the schooling turns into a verbal charade. For an adult, in contrast, the sheer amount of experience he has shared in is some protection against the school's tendency toward rationalism and verbalism. In an adult's life, questions, decisions and actions have been encountered and resolved in one way or another. Now the gentle voice of reason has a chance of being heard as it reflects upon this experience. Reason used in this fashion will be at the service of intelligence, enriching experience by ordering it and freeing man by integrating him.

This long section on education and schooling was necessary

15. See Randy Huntsberry, "Learning Without Authority," in *The Religious Situation*: 1969, ed. Donald Cutler (Boston, 1969), pp. 755–762; also Thomas Kuhn, *The Structure of Scientific Revolutions* (Chicago, 1962).

16. Newmann and Oliver, *loc. cit.*, p. 219.

before the question of religious or ecumenical education could be correctly posed. Even if some of the above principles seem utopian or romantic in light of the present school scene, they are still correct principles for elaborating a theory on the proper structure of ecumenical education. Two important points can be noted immediately. First, in the above discussion of schooling and education, the process of education was described as co-extensive with humanization. Education, as the use of all means which move forward the project of greater freedom, wholeness and creativity for mankind, is a lifelong task. Schooling, on the other hand, is a particular instrument of varying worth depending on the age, background and total context of education. Some schooling at some times can be instrumental to education. Schools can also be at times a hindrance to education. It would follow that an ecumenical or religious education is a lifelong work. However, it is a different question to ask when, if ever, religion should be taught in schools. It is a still different question whether churches should conduct schools and if so for whom. I am not against religious education for children. Indeed, I am in favor of beginning an ecumenical education pre-natally and extending it to preparation for death by old age. How much religion should be taught in school involves other issues.

Second, the sharp distinction between education and schooling may seem unrealistic in twentieth century America because of our recent hopes and the continuing rhetoric. Is there any evidence that education can be effective in other ways than through the school? To this question the churches might be able to contribute something from their own experience which even if not scientifically controlled is at least long and varied. The religious education wing of the churches is still almost entirely child centered and school centered. Everything revolves around the children or the adults' relation to children. This arrangement, even for the children themselves, is an inefficient and unhealthy one. But there is another side to the church's educational work which is not called religious education but which may actually be the effective education in the churches. From the earliest days of the church there has been some realization that the way to understand Christianity is to live it. Education in Christianity has been provided by contemplative and liturgical prayer, the guidance of the family, the experience of the community and action for social justice. This tradition of "Christian education" has been a rich one and, though more neglected than adverted to over the centuries, has never died out. Education in general might learn something from this Christian practice.

The aim of ecumenical education is the same as education itself, namely, the lived truth of a humanized world. The ecumenical is not a part of education with a separate set of objectives nor an addition to an otherwise incomplete education. The ecumenical refers to a way of specifying or concretizing the truth by presenting the religious alternatives that life offers. My presumption is that questions of final meaning, symbolism, ritual and claims for total commitment arise in every life. The intention of this book is not to prescribe that people must accept a religious belief and ritual but that this issue ought to be intelligently dealt with in education.

When the question of religion is placed into the narrow context of the school, there are further practical issues involved. Compromises, adjustments and transitional policies may influence what is actually done in the school. Religion ought of its nature to bring the emotional and rational into an intelligent union but a study of religion that would accomplish this feat presupposes that much else has been studied. Religion, I shall claim, should not be a course of study in one's early schooling.

There may be a temporary role, however, for religion classes in a school. The religion course may keep alive certain questions not only about God but about human values and social structures. At least for the short term the work of religious teaching may be largely one of compensating for deficiencies in general education. If education in human values is not going on in history or social science, then a religion class could serve this

85

purpose. If literature is not being appreciated in English literature class, then perhaps the literature can be read in conjunction with a religion course. As a matter of fact, this is what is happening in many Catholic schools where there are sensitive religion teachers. Religion class has become the time of the day when students can say what they feel and can ask questions which the school otherwise avoids. It is a remarkable turnabout when religion classes become such forums of free expression. Such classes may not be typical of all the religion classes in the system. Nonetheless, many religion teachers are making a worthwhile contribution, usually under some pressure, in opening their classes to whatever concerns the students.[17]

While expressing some admiration for this development in Catholic schools, I am doubtful about the long term future of these courses. Those who are engaged in teaching religion in Catholic schools ought to be aware of the precariousness of their role. A compensatory role is one which should be eliminated as soon as is possible. When religion courses exercise the role well, they will eventually change the general attitude of the school and consequently make such a course unnecessary. Where education is of high quality in a school, the maintenance of a religion class throughout the school will tend to become superfluous. If there is a role for religion in formal education, a role that does not tend toward its own phasing out, it will have to be something other than talking about student problems, reading novels and watching movies. I think that religion can and should have a permanent role in education, as part of a course in lower levels of education and as a full course of study in higher education. I will try to describe this place but first it might be contrasted with attempts to teach religion to a small child.

For reasons both theological and educational I think that it is impossible to teach a religion course to a child. I would go

17. See Robert Wicks, "A Space for Reflection," in *Religious Education,* 64 (Mar./Apr., 1969), pp. 104–107.

further and claim that most such attempts are disasters and that the reason there is not worse disaster is because the teaching is often productive of no results at all. Even with well prepared teachers and the most up to date textbooks the attempts cannot work because of the subject matter. I would reiterate that a small child is a very religious being who needs plenty of religious education but a course on religion is almost certain to be inimical to that education. The kind of course that can be taught is simply not the kind of religion that a child needs.

In the main line of church tradition, the religious education of children has never been noted for any qualities like creativity, open-mindedness and toleration of uncertainty. The finished products of thousand year discussions are provided for the nourishment of six-year-olds. Whatever may be the beauties of logic and verbal artistry, and in fact precisely because of these characteristics, a small child is quite overwhelmed by the biblical and Christian doctrines taught in the schools. Thus, it is, wrote Sebastian Moore, "that Catholic religion can have, *materialiter,* the same effect on the young as the vast mass of salacious literature available on all bookstalls for this is nothing but a commercial racket for keeping us all at the adolescent stage."[18]

The harsh sounding metaphor that Moore uses may not be far from the mark. Flannery O'Connor used to say that most Catholics seem capable of recognizing only the sentimental and the obscene; they prefer the first and are upset by the second.[19] What they do not realize is the close connection between the two of them. Both spring from the unhealthy separation of emotion and the critical function of reason. A course of religion for children is incapable of keeping these two together; it lacks all the necessary space to build gradually toward an ultimate integrity.

18. Sebastian Moore, *God Is a New Language* (Westminster, Md., 1967), p. 22.
19. See Flannery O'Connor, *Mystery and Manners* (New York, 1969), p. 147.

A course of religion for children is in proximate danger of having three effects. First, there is a complete failure in understanding but an apparently profound understanding when children can repeat religious truths. Summing up Ronald Goldman's studies of religion teaching, Harold Loukes writes: "For the majority of our schoolchildren, therefore, the whole of their religious instruction is nothing but a course of instruction in knowledge-without-meaning: it is the delivery of loads of bricks to a site on which, until they are about to leave, they have no equipment for building."[20] The bricks, it should be noted, not only do not make the building but they present an obstacle to getting the equipment to build. This oversaturation is directly connected to the other two dangerous results: sentimentality and prejudice.

Sentimentality, I have already noted, is the exploitation of emotion apart from critical reason. Because religion is supposed to arouse feeling and action while as a matter of fact the dry doctrines of belief do not arouse either, there are practically always sentimental considerations supplemental to the course. Religion that should be a striving to awaken the highest critical faculties often contributes to what seems to be a general American tendency toward sentimentality. This characteristic may be a more serious failing than we are accustomed to think. "The net result of sentimentality is to shift the American psyche away from a critical approach to the problems of community and to the standards of quality that should obtain in the community. For the question of quality is in large part a question of taste and questions of taste are largely based on measured emotion, gauged passion. When feeling is either held all inside, or is turned upon the world in a flood of anger or love (more often love), no measure, no matching up, no critical test is possible. Americans for the most part cannot tell good music from bad, good art from

20. Harold Loukes, *New Ground in Christian Education* (London, 1965), p. 61.

bad, not because of unintelligence but because of the overkill of diffused, generalized sentiment."[21]

The other dangerous tendency of teaching religion to those unprepared for it is that of producing prejudice and intolerance. The studies of Gordon Allport indicated, and more recent studies confirm, that religion badly assimilated increases prejudice.[22] Allport always distinguished between two kinds of religion according to the way religion functions in an individual life. It is important to know whether religion functions intrinsically or extrinsically, whether it has been assimilated organically or has been adopted as a defense against experience. Allport's distinction is not unrelated to the distinctions about religion that I made in chapter two. There is an immature religion and a mature religion and "nothing is more inadequate than a mature judgment when adopted by an immature mind" (Goethe). The attempt to teach religion to those unprepared for it causes a block in growth which is at the root of prejudice. "Prejudice itself is a matter of stereotyped overgeneralization, a failure to distinguish members of a minority group as individuals. It goes without saying that if categories are overwide the accompanying feeling tone will be undifferentiated . . . It seems probable that people with undifferentiated styles of thinking (and feeling) are not entirely secure in a world that for the most part demands fine and accurate distinctions. The resulting diffuse anxiety may well dispose them to grapple on to religion and to distrust strange ethnic groups."[23]

The tendencies toward prejudice and sentimentality are not mainly the result of wrong intentions, bad textbooks or poor teaching. Nor can the problems be corrected by tinkering with

21. Sellers, *op. cit.,* p. 174.
22. See Gordon Allport, *The Person in Psychology* (Boston, 1968), pp. 187–263; Robert Brannon, "Gimme That Old Time Religion," in *Psychology Today,* 3 (Spring, 1970) pp. 42–44.
23. Allport, *op. cit.,* p. 259 f.

the books or the teachers. The problem is endemic to the system. Large-scale change must be undertaken to counteract negative results in the system that now exists. What I have tried to do so far in this book is to set the background for proposing an "ecumenical curriculum," that is, a course for education in religion from birth to grave. I would first like to put it in the form of a diagram and then explain it further.

primitive religion	narrow Christianity	ecumenical religion/Christianity
primitive intellect	reason	mature intelligence
body skills family care play arts stories	science ——— comparative history ———／ religion literature ／	(Christian) theology

In the remaining pages of this chapter, I will only comment on the nature of the diagram. The following two chapters will deal with the individual pieces of the diagram. It should be kept in mind that this is a proposed sequence to arrive at an intelligent understanding of the religious aspects of human life. The diagram is constructed by a Christian using certain Christian presuppositions; it makes no claim to being ecumenically perfect. However, I do not believe that anyone can speak in this area without making some presuppositions. One escapes bias not by avoiding presuppositions but by making them known. In any case, this book is addressed to a specific audience at a particular moment. The proposed curriculum represents a quantum leap from where we are without losing continuity with the past. If a Buddhist were to look at the diagram, I presume that he would not accept it as his own but I would hope that it could be at least one basis for discussion.

As the completion of the process I have listed (Christian) theology to indicate that if Christianity is the free and intelligent choice of the adult, then the study of theology is proper to adulthood. I have put the word Christian in parentheses to indicate that this sequence, *even on Christian premises,* may lead to some other religion. I am claiming that a mature intelligence will somehow pursue religious inquiry.

I am aware that the use of the word theology may have two distinct disadvantages. From the Christian side, theology is often considered to be a technical, professional, academic enterprise. In Catholic circles it is usually distinguished from catechesis which is understood to be a communication of faith for believers. From the non-Christian side, theology as a *logos* of God is often considered to be a peculiarly Christian enterprise and even one of an Hellenic Christianity.

In reference to the first point I have used theology to emphasize that the split between theology and catechesis is unfortunate. Undoubtedly, one could historically and methodologically justify a distinction between the two words, but the split that actually exists is completely misleading. There should not be catechesis for children and theology for seminarians. Catechetical and theological education are the same thing; both pertain to the communication, understanding and assimilation of Christian faith. I could have used the word catechesis in my diagram where I used theology but people would find it difficult to take the term in a fully adult context. However, if the word is to be retained at all it belongs here. In other words, children are not to be catechized at all. Both words, theology and catechesis, have their troubles, but I judge the former to be more salvageable than the latter.

Regarding the non-Christian objection to the term theology I can only say that the word is used to designate mature understanding of faith for a Christian. It does not connote one method or one particular relationship to philosophy. Theology is intended to designate that a person, after a long personal development and some comparison, has chosen to get on the inside of a tradition and to understand and live it on its own terms. This

91

does not mean that the person leaves the outside world and no longer tests the truth of his religion by its relation to subsequent experience. It does mean that without some personal involvement, some living from the inside out, there can be little intelligent appreciation of a religion. A term like "religious inquiry" does not convey that flavor. If "theology" is not acceptable in some traditions, it is up to them to describe the process in other ways.

In the first two columns I have listed some educational activities; the lists could be extended indefinitely. They are meant merely to indicate some sequence in these activities. I have not attempted to place age limits on this sequence although this could be done fairly easily. I prefer to talk about the educational activities themselves and this will indicate the age span. Developmental psychology could set some upper and lower limits. Learning to speak is obviously an activity of a small child but studying history is not. Where and how history should be studied involves many considerations which are not germane here.

Whatever differences of detail might exist, psychology and common sense would agree that there is a stage of life when a person is immersed in immediate experience and is taken care of by some adult. The child's education at this point is pre-analytic, pre-reflective and pre-rational. The ecumenical education of the child at this age consists in whatever is humanly helpful in his growing up. As I shall try to indicate in the next chapter, there is a great deal more here than many people would suspect at first sight. There is plenty of the religious in the child's experience though it may have little to do with what some adults think of as religion.

On the line between the first and second stage I have put the word arts. The synthesizing of these stages is an important point which I shall come back to shortly. The word arts retains some bond with the pre-rational but it also includes some move toward the controlled use of song, play, dance and material. The word literature could have been included with the arts but because of its verbal character, and consequently its unique position in many religions, I have placed it over with science and history.

My point in regard to this second column is that the study of these human developments is a further progress in understanding the religious life of man. I am also indicating that there is an historical connection between a somewhat narrow or reactive Christianity and the development of science, technology and history in the West. To study physics is to meet in some small way the effect of Christian belief, that is, the demystification of the ancient world and the expansion of human freedom to change everything. History and literature, from a different direction, are also in part the teaching of religion because the work of religion is embedded in the study itself. The study of history, for example, should include units on religion simply because this is an important part of history. Church education has usually been biased by its highly selective inclusion of religious elements in history. Public education has usually been biased by its exclusion of all religious issues.

On the second line I have placed comparative religion. It would emerge from studies in the second column but it is moving into a final stage of religious understanding. A very systematic study that can legitimately be called "comparative religion" may not be possible but the principle of comparativeness cannot be neglected. There should be admission and appreciation of the fact that there are alternate ways to understand religion. If the religious questions are approached in their normal anthropological setting, this understanding should not be difficult to achieve. Of course, such a study is not meant for an eight-year-old. The study of religion as an isolated phenomenon presupposes a wide spectrum of previous study.

There is, finally, a study from within one's own religious tradition. With background secured and freedom not pressured, a person should be able to find sustenance for his life in such study. Some people may think that this study of Christian theology is postponed too long. But if one is thinking in the framework of a seventy-year educational span, it is still rather early in the process.

A final remark must be made here about the legitimacy of a three-stage sequence. The very word sequence may give the impression that the second replaces the first and the third is a substitution for both of the preceding. In Chapters 2 and 3 I stressed the point that the third picks up the best elements in the first and the second. Ecumenical religion is neither post-Christian nor part Christian but a religious way of being Christian and a Christian way of being religious. Likewise, adult understanding is neither rational nor irrational nor a little of each. It is a way of being toward the world that subsumes the rational and irrational within an attitude that accepts the complex world.

The educational pattern, therefore, is a rhythm in which one moves through a sequence where the third element has to synthesize what appear to be contradictory elements. Philosophers from Plato to Whitehead have seen this as the great task of education.[24] In Whitehead's delightful description, he points to three stages called romance, precision and generalization. He traces this movement through a day, a year, a lifetime so that large movements have smaller movements within them, like eddies in a current of water. He also emphasizes that in any one phase, the other two phases ought not to be excluded but should form a background. There are times for the hard work of precise analysis but not so exclusively that all sense of romance is lost.

This brief reflection would indicate how theology is to come about and what should be some of its qualities. Without losing the discursive, scientific and controlled elements of its development, it has to pick up some of the wonder, fantasy and mystery which are also in its background. If theology is out of touch with the roots of human life it quickly becomes a closed world

24. See Charles Stinnette, *Learning in Theological Perspective* (New York, 1965), p. 26; A. N. Whitehead, *The Aims of Education* (New York, 1949), pp. 27–51.

94

strangling on its own jargon. Perhaps more than any other study, theology must recognize the limits of its language and keep re-immersing itself into more primitive experiences of life, love and language.

For this reason the arts bear the heaviest burden in preparing the way for theology and in keeping it in touch with reality. The arts prevent the rational and the nonrational from getting too far apart. When it comes to the most perfected form of communication it will be an artistic one. We have passed through a time when the discipline of theology was a rigid and inhuman logic of sources and hair-splitting to a time when theology is somewhat chaotic in its allusions to movies or literature. We will have come home when theology has a drama to itself and with the discipline of an artist draws together a vast range of human resources to demonstrate that there are unthought surprises in our present and future.

5. Ecumenical Education for Pre-Adults

THE use of the word pre-adult in the title of this chapter indicates the wide span of years that is to be dealt with in this chapter. Besides being a comprehensive word, pre-adult also suggests the method by which the process is to be defined. These years have their meaning in relation to the adulthood toward which they move. This perspective is not a return to the old error of disregarding a child's immediate feelings and providing him with bits of learning that would supposedly help him later in life. An infant or a youth has a life of his own that must be respected. But to respect a person growing up is to recognize that his being is a being in process and the process cannot be understood without reference to its culmination.

For this reason it was difficult to decide whether or not to reverse Chapters 5 and 6. The ecumenical education of the pre-adult is in some ways unintelligible outside of the intrinsic relation which it has to adult religious education. However, I am presuming that this general framework has already been established. This chapter merely expands on individual elements of this framework.

It would be pretentious to try to make any worthwhile comment within the space of a few pages on the place of art, science or history in education. I wish to make clear the very restricted purpose of these comments. I am not trying to explain the place of the humanities in the university or the role of music education in elementary schools. I am only pointing out connections between education in religion and other educational experiences which are apparently nonreligious. In some cases the connection may be fairly direct and obvious; for example, the study of history should include study of the religions of mankind. In other cases, the connection is more indirect and open to debate; for example, the study of science is the cultivation of attitudes that in history are consequent to Christian belief and for an individual today are antecedent to Christian belief.

These two examples point up the dynamisms of the complicated process I am trying to get at. Both of these connections to religious belief are important but the second, that is, the indirect one, is more important in the long run. If this second one does not come into play at all then the first one will become dull, lifeless and probably nonexistent in public education; and naive, proselytizing and probably corruptive in church education. If religion is something that is simply inserted into courses, the result will not be worth the effort. But if this effort is accompanied by a concern with how every subject is taught and how education operates in a community, then we will really be on the way to an ecumenical education.

What I mean can be clarified by admitting the theological premise from which I work. The thesis maintained throughout this book is that Christianity is an invitation to human intelligence and freedom to re-create the world. I am claiming that in Christianity there need not be any authorities that are simply external and consequently repressive. Power and authority reside in earthly man and his openness to the infinite. There are views of Christianity, both past and present, which run counter to this view. I am not denying the painful realities of some of the church's past nor am I making exorbitant claims about Christianity's present. I am asserting that if Christian faith has a future it will issue from a way of looking at the world that stimulates response, creativity and passionate involvement. Any education that encourages such attitudes is an education that is already on the way to a point where Christian faith *can* be accepted. There is no guarantee that Christian faith will be the outcome of such education, but, if it is not, we can expect an alternative way that intelligently deals with ultimate human questions. Any education, in contrast, that does not encourage creativeness, curiosity, discovery, excitement, wonder and joy is not moving toward the acceptance of Christian faith no matter what is being taught.

It is not just in a few selected fields that a child can be taught creativity. Creativity is always being learned in any good educational process because of the way in which the process occurs. Education in anything at any level involves man's most profound attitude toward the whole world, an attitude that the church tradition calls creatureliness.[1] In this regard there should be a reciprocal relation between creativity and Christian belief. The church could consistently remind man that he is neither god nor the devil but simply man, the creature. Referring to the plight of a young person in a noncreated world, Paul Goodman writes: "Not being a creature, with its awe and humility, he does not dare to be open to the creative spirit, to become himself on occasion a creator. If, by exception, he does create something, he is conceited about it and contemptuous of the others, as if it were his; and conversely, he is gnawed by fear that he will lose the power, as if it were something he had. A society that so discourages the young has nothing to recommend it."[2]

In connecting a mature religious outlook and basic educational attitudes, I am equating (at least for early life) religious education and good education. This equation is one which not all people in education would accept or need accept. My purpose is not to convince all educators that they are really religious educators. I am more concerned with convincing people, who advocate religious education for children, that they ought to be concerned with education.

There is a point in the educational process when religion can be studied and there is a time for pursuing a theological grasp of Christianity, but that time is not in childhood. At that time of

1. See Gabriel Moran, "Creative Spirit,'" in *Colloquy,* 2 (Dec., 1969), pp. 6–7.
2. Paul Goodman, *Growing Up Absurd* (New York, 1956), pp. 148 f.

life religion is too important to be confined to a subject in school. The religious attitude is diffused through a child's experience. The isolation of the religious element for the purpose of interpretation would make it cease to be religious. There are profound religious questions that all children raise. Paul Tillich tells a story about his daughter when she was six years old. "We were walking through an Alpine meadow and suddenly she asked, 'Why is all this so? Here is the meadow, there the trees and there the mountain. Why isn't it all different?' "[3] The literature of the centuries reveals that it is not only the small Tillichs who ask such questions. However, theology and psychology, if not common sense, should tell us that even six-year-old Tillichs are not proved ready for their father's systematic theology when they ask such questions.

In denying that any course on Christianity can be taught to a child, it may seem that I am opposing the well-known dictum of Jerome Bruner's that "any subject can be taught effectively in some intellectually honest form to any child at any stage of development."[4] On the contrary, I am subscribing to this principle and looking for the "honest form" of ecumenical education. The assumption is still widespread, especially among textbook people, that with more research, experiments and hard work, the Christian religion can be taught to children. The reason why I flatly deny this assumption is because I deny that Christianity is a subject of study. There is indeed a subject to be studied which should be called religion. The relation of Christianity to religion, as I have tried to show, is a complicated one. In one sense religion precedes Christianity and in another sense of the word religion is wider than Christianity. The course of studies I am trying to describe, therefore, is not one which has Christianity as its subject but one which is the ecumenical study of religion. Such a course of studies may seem unnecessary to some Christians but from the point of view of *formal education* it is the only

3. Paul Tillich, *Ultimate Concern* (New York, 1965), p. 194.
4. Jerome Bruner, *The Process of Education* (New York, 1963), p. 33.

way into Christianity. There may indeed be better ways of getting into the church than going through a school but if one is talking about a school then the preparation for being a Christian is to appreciate art as art, history as history, and science as science.

The last statement would obviate the objection that a person should not be prevented from being a Christian until he is an adult and has gone through a long course of study of secular subjects. This is not the necessary consequence of what I am advocating. I presume that children will continue to be born into Catholic families and that they will absorb whatever Christian attitudes and practices are operating in the home. However, adults must realize that children have lives of their own built from the base of their own experience. If they are finally to live as followers of Christ and members of the church, they must grow into this style of life at their own pace. Thus, there should be no ban on exposure to Christian literature, symbolism and practice. In fact, all children in our society should have an acquaintance with and appreciation of Christianity. Correlatively, no child should be considered to be a full-fledged member of the church until he has acquired an appreciation of Christianity in relation to other religious and non-religious options. It must be emphasized that such a slowly developing appreciation does not come from taking a neutral stand outside the phenomenon nor is it likely to come wholly from courses in school. The appreciation arises from being immersed in a community experience which provides material for reflection but does not prevent critical reason from coming to bear on the experience.

The description in the following pages of some aspects of formal education presupposes the experience of community that precedes and accompanies them. Education ought to be a process in which the whole community educates the whole community for the whole of communal life. A major part of education's problem today is the breakdown of community in its traditional form. There are attempts today to find new forms of community that would make up at least in part for the former values. Without some form of community experience, no educational venture will be successful and an ecumenical education is doubly handicapped.

The key element in the educational process is the presence of community. The direction and attitudes toward learning are set very early in life. "It is astonishing at what an early age a baby cries not because of any psychological distress, but because he has noticed that he is alone, and is upset by his mother's absence."[5] It is through the experience of this other's love that a child develops a sense of trust and also experiences his own worth and dignity. In order to learn anything well he has to experience that it is "safe to be transparently real."[6] If children have approached learning in this way from their earliest years then the process of formal education will reflect this attitude of confidence, trust and searching inquiry. John Holt, in trying to describe the difference between bright children and "slow learners," writes: "It seems as if what we call intelligent children feel that the universe can be trusted even when it does not seem to make any sense, that even when you don't understand it you can be fairly sure that it is not going to play dirty tricks on you."[7] When psychological threat to the organism is low, then change of behavior and new learning are possible. A person must experience his unique worth as reflected in the eyes of another before his own universe can be looked at, accepted, understood and changed.[8]

A church group could make an invaluable contribution to education by contributing some experience of community. I have pointed out that one reason for having a religion time for children would be to make up for deficiencies in general educa-

5. John MacMurray, *Persons in Relation* (London, 1961), p. 49.
6. Rogers, *On Becoming a Person*, p. 51.
7. John Holt, *How Children Fail* (New York, 1964), p. 46.
8. See Charles A. Curran, *Religious Values in Counseling and Psychotherapy* (New York, 1969), p. 35; Carl Rogers, *Freedom to Learn* (Columbus, 1969), p. 161; E. Schein and W. Bennis, *Personal and Organizational Change Through Group Methods* (New York, 1965), p. 276.

tion. The deficiencies of education are not restricted to the content of courses. Contributions are needed in more ways than what is taught in history or social science. The chief deficiency in education is the number of people who are willing to get involved or who are capable of contributing a communal experience. What many students in educational institutions need is to run up against human beings who will challenge them and discipline them.

The church in its eagerness to explain things tends to overlook itself as a resource. One reason for this omission is the realization or suspicion on the part of the church that, despite verbal claims to being a community, the preconditions of community experience are lacking. A number of people living together or working together is not a community. Only when there is a network of human relationships that are unleashing the human energies which heal and reveal does one have a communion of persons. Sometimes an individual religion teacher or a particular church group does succeed in providing a community experience. A religion course may then be successful aside from what is taught and even possibly in spite of what is taught. This limited achievement is hardly a matter for unrestrained rejoicing but its significance should not be entirely discounted, either. Harold Loukes, summarizing his study of the best religion teaching he could find, writes: "The boys and girls knew themselves to be loved. These classes were without fear: relaxed, unhurried, often a little bored, but contented. I can imagine that when they leave school . . . they will recall their school days and say, Well I couldn't understand what they were talking about, and I still don't; but they were on my side."[9]

At the earliest stages of human life there is a perfect identity between education and ecumenical education. The one clear and unequivocal message of Christianity to parents is that they should provide the best conditions for letting the child grow up. Presumably many parents could and do follow this policy without

9. Loukes, *op. cit.*, pp. 90 f.

any encouragement from Christianity, but the added support should be to their advantage. At the least it would eliminate negative attitudes in infant care that religion sometimes encouraged under its doctrine of sin. Adults need all the help they can get in trusting a child's emotional growth, aggressiveness and independence.

Infancy is a time for setting the direction of emotional and affective life. I have called it the stage of "primitive intelligence," that is, a pre-rational and pre-analytical phase of growth. The genius of child education, Maria Montessori, has written at length on this topic: "Formerly it was thought that the small child had no psychic life, whereas now we realize that the only part of him which is active during the first year is the brain! The chief characteristic of the human babe is intelligence, unlike the other animals who only need to awaken the instinct toward their behavior. The human child's intelligence has to take in the present of an evolving life which goes back hundreds of thousands of years in its civilization, and which has stretching before it a future of millions of years."[10] The active power to learn is already in the smallest infant and enables the child to perform the incredibly complicated tasks of eating, walking and talking.

A small child needs a guarantee that it is all right to feel, to experience, to be curious and to learn. Besides the exciting and joyful dimensions of infant experience there are always elements of threat and danger somewhere in the environment, whether the child is growing up in an African jungle or downtown Brooklyn. Thus, there is the need for an adult guarantor of experience. Unfortunately, the exigencies of parenthood being what they are, the process of affective growth never succeeds perfectly. Children are cut short in their curiosity and sometimes even punished for it. The fears, ignorance and hatred of an adult population conspire against the emotional life of the child.

A child begins with an "organismic valuing process" in which

10. Maria Montessori, *Education for a New World* (Madras, 1959), p. 31.

a thing is valued by whether at this moment it actualizes the organism.[11] Very quickly, however, adult standards are interjected into the process so that some feelings and statements are called "nice" and are rewarded while other genuine human feelings are called bad and are banished by edict. The edicts, of course, do not work because feelings do not disappear; they simply submerge and reappear in distorted shape. Education for a small child should be the aiding of awareness, acceptance and expression of his feelings. The educating adults not only fail to do this, but often they conceive of their job as the very opposite, that is, of selecting which feelings should exist, of judging which ones are good and of restricting the expression of those that are judged bad. Haim Ginott writes: "Many people have been educated out of knowing what their feelings are. When they hated, they were told it was only dislike. When they were afraid, they were told there was nothing to be afraid of. When they felt pain they were advised to be brave and smile. Many of our popular songs tell us 'Pretend you are happy when you are not.' What is suggested in the place of this pretense? Truth. Emotional education can help children to *know what they feel.* It is more important for a child to know what he feels than why he feels it. When he knows what his feelings are, he is less likely to feel 'all mixed-up' inside."[12]

The underlying feeling which is most suspect in children is aggressiveness with its concomitant assertion of individuality and independence. Other feelings are tolerable because the adult world can still believe in its complete power over the child, sometimes camouflaged as over caring love and at other times openly expressed as envy and fright. "The word *no,* for a two year old, is the Declaration of Independence and Magna Carta rolled into one. Oddly enough, most people seem alarmed by the first stages of independence in small children. Modern parents often say, 'It's just a stage, they'll grow out of it,' as if it

11. See Rogers, *Freedom to Learn,* p. 242.
12. Haim Ginott, *Between Parent and Child* (New York, 1967), p. 35.

were a disease from which, with care and luck, the child might recover. The more old-fashioned ones set out to show the tiny child Who Is Boss, though the child feels completely dependent and though his desire for greater independence needs all the nourishment it can get."[13]

The alternative to "breaking their wills" is not unbridled permissiveness; these two in fact usually go together. The genuine educating process is one of interaction and dialogue. "Nature" does not guarantee a rich human development; the full range of human potential can only be brought out by other human beings. "Falls bruise, glass breaks, animals yelp or run or bite. Parents should provide a superior environment, one capable of laughing, crying, galumphing, sympathizing, and stomping the floor in righteous indignation."[14] The assertion of adult individuality in a firm and definite way is part of the process of cultivating the child's individuality.

Adults must and do carry out some kind of process of selection and evaluation in the child's behavior. There is nothing wrong with this action so long as the adult is trying to participate in a judgment which the child is making on his own experience. The most common failure of adults is to praise or condemn the child instead of evaluating particular behavior. Parents often say "you are bad" or "you are stupid" and the child may begin to believe it, particularly because the adults' judgments can be buttressed by rewards and punishments. "The single most important rule is that praise deal only with the child's efforts and accomplishments, *not* with his character and personality."[15] Many adults are careful not to be harsh and condemnatory toward children but they tend to over praise them. "Curiously enough, a positive evaluation is as threatening in the long run as a nega-

13. John Holt, *How Children Learn* (New York, 1967), p. 23.
14. Kenneth Eble, *A Perfect Education* (New York, 1966), p. 16; see also Jean Piaget, *The Moral Judgment of the Child* (New York, 1962), p. 404; Anthony Storr, *Human Aggression* (New York, 1968), p. 45.
15. Ginott, *op. cit.,* p. 39.

tive one, since to inform someone that he is good implies that you also have the right to tell him he is bad."[16]

Parents would do best to accept the human animal as fundamentally good but always fallible. If they were to accept that premise for themselves as well as for their children, they could live with fewer pretenses and an authority grounded in truth. They would probably find that their children would not always be easy to work with but that each problem could be dealt with inside of a standing framework of trust.

The chief educational activity in the stage of primitive intellect is play. Beginning in infancy and emerging as central to childhood, play is an element that should never be lost from life. The role of mature intelligence, as I have previously described it, is to incorporate or reintegrate the element of primitive intellect into rational life. By that standard an intelligent man is necessarily a playful man. "The sense of play, discovery, and order, fully developed and not allowed to atrophy, give a beginning for acquiring a sense of style. One cannot free himself enough from any of the demands of life to show grace or to inspire imitation without the sense of play . . . An individual's nature is seldom attractive if it does not show some sense of play. An ability to let up, to squander time profitably, seems characteristic of those who have acquired style in living."[17] Play, therefore, is not an indulgence which has to be outgrown but a central fact of all learning. A knowledgeable person is one who can make sport with what he knows and give creative rein to his fancy in changing the world. There is no reason why the play element should disappear completely in the learning of anything at any level.

The question of play is very serious business. It cuts far deeper than educational techniques and reveals something pro-

16. Carl Rogers, "The Characteristics of a Helping Relationship," in *The Planning of Change*, ed. Warren Bennis, Kenneth Benne, Robert Chin (New York, 1969), p. 165.
17. Eble, *op. cit.*, pp. 178 f.

found about the nature of man. At this point, the particular significance of play for ecumenical education becomes apparent. Play is the natural way in which man comes to understand himself as a creature and grasps how he is to live in the universe about him. It is not by accident that play sneaks back into adult life through the two avenues of religion and making love. Wherever man is most fully himself, play is not absent; the existence of play is the revealing of man who can be more than he thinks. When we get to heaven, wrote Horace Bushnell, our occupation can be nothing else than play. A theology that truly understands the implications of play comes closest to understanding man's relation to God, the solidity and yet fragility of the world, and the divine humor which is sometimes wry but never cruel. Hugo Rahner, in his book *Man at Play,* has worked out some of the theological implications of playful man. "He must be a man who neither cynically despises the world nor is consumed by an epicurean appetite for it; he must be a man who has the divine so much at the center of his preoccupations that he can find it in the things of this world. In other words, the nature of the inward gaiety of the man who truly plays, and for whom earnest and jest are sisters, is at bottom a religious problem, and this peculiar quality can only be attained by one who is both of heaven and of earth."[18]

The play of children manifests itself in games and stories, both of which reveal the finiteness of man and his dreams of the infinite. In games a child can learn the connection between play and rules; he can begin to learn to set limits on anticipated consequences of activities. It is unfortunate that adults interfere so often in this process to set up the rules or prevent their breakdown.[19] The experience of team play in games provides a child with a paradigm of life's joys and sorrows, death and resurrection. Games allow passionate emotional involvement. While inviting

18. Hugo Rahner, *Man at Play* (New York, 1967), p. 35.
19. See the remarkable illustration recounted in Dennison, *op. cit.,* pp. 201 f.; also Bruner, *Toward a Theory of Instruction,* pp. 134–147.

expression of feeling in the public arena, they respect the privacy of the individual. It has sometimes been said that the thing which American education does best is to produce athletic teams, a fact which should not be very surprising considering that these teams build on the propensities of the young whereas nearly all of formal education runs counter to learning through team play. "In this respect," writes anthropologist George Pettitt, "contemporary adult hominids sometimes act less intelligently than a band of baboons, where peer groups are an accepted part of the social organization and provide the only highly socialized, liberal education that a baboon gets."[20]

The ecumenical significance of stories is even more evident than games. All religions have involved stories about the gods and the marvelous interaction of the human and the divine. Sorrow can be borne so long as it can be placed in a story. Hope can survive so long as men can dream of a better world. Children do not have to be supplied with "religious stories"; their ordinary stories bristle with religious depths if adults can appreciate them. A child's perception of the wonders and surprises of the universe can be expressed in the language of a story because the story can heighten joy and channel off fear. The sacred text of any religion is full of wonderful stories that appeal to the mind of a child.

The tragedy is that adults can easily mistake the significance of story telling and take it to be merely a childish thing. It is assumed that a rational and scientific explanation is always preferable and more accurate than a grand story about the human and the divine, that is, a myth. The word myth had fallen into such disrepute that it was almost a synonym for falsehood, opposed as it was to history and to fact. Even while the meaning of myth was being rediscovered, Christian theology went through a period of "de-mythologizing." Rudolf Bultmann probably did not intend what that somewhat ill chosen word seems to indi-

20. George Pettitt, *Prisoners of Culture* (New York, 1970), pp. 110 f.

cate.[21] Nevertheless, many people in recent years have presumed that Christianity should get rid of myths and everything that had the scent of a mythical element. The tide has recently swung, however, and a new appreciation of the truth value of the mythical is emerging. It is not a new exegesis of Bultmann that has done it but a rediscovery of the capacity of a story to convey what a rational, discursive and analytical mode of speech cannot get at. If, as Baudelaire said, genius is the rediscovery of childhood, it is because the adult who is in touch with life discovers that his childhood myths have a truth that transcends reason. Paul Ricoeur, who has examined at length the role of symbol and myth, writes: "By its triple function of concrete universality, temporal orientation, and finally ontological exploration, the myth has a way of *revealing* things that is not reducible to any translation from the language in cipher to a clear language."[22]

Games and stories are the prelude to the set of experiences grouped under the word arts. In the terminology used here the arts (music, painting, sculpture, film, drama) are distinct from both the humanities and the sciences. The arts, as indicated in the diagram of Chapter 4, have the crucial role of binding the pre-rational and the rational. Artistic expression ought to precede discursive studies and form a continuing background for rational explorations. There is an aesthetic element not only in the humanities but in the sciences, and the aesthetic experience makes possible the synthesis of mature intelligence. If enactive and iconic forms of learning are not preserved throughout the entire educative process, then men will eventually be faced with the choice between brutalized instinctual drives and repressive rationalized systems. "In the end works of art are the only media of complete and unhindered communication between man and man

21. See Rudolf Bultmann, *Jesus Christ and Mythology* (New York, 1958); for a summary of the question, see Robert Neale, *In Praise of Play* (New York, 1969), pp. 129–146.
22. See Gilkey, *op. cit.,* p. 391.

that can occur in a world full of gulfs and walls that limit community of experience . . . The sense of communion generated by a work may take on a definitely religious quality. The union of men with one another is the source of the rites that from the time of archaic man to the present have commemorated the crises of birth, death and marriage."[23]

The main point I wish to stress concerning art is that the aesthetic experience itself is revelational of the human and divine. Religious education has in recent years discovered the film, novel and photograph; and has made "use" of them to teach religion. The difficulty is in the word "use" because the arts used merely as a vehicle to teach about God are almost certain to teach neither the aesthetic nor the divine. Instead of seeing movies that have a religious message, children would be better off seeing any movie that is aesthetically well done. They might be still better off if they were making their own movies.

Any discussion on the teaching of the arts should include a reflection that teaching itself is an art and must have an aesthetic quality to it. "The teacher, then, in classroom activity can tame the incipient chaos and dominate it with human intelligence. Classroom activity can seem ready to disintegrate but for the aesthetic order imposed by the teacher. The influence of this ordered disorder upon the student, if it is an object or event of beauty, is not to make him mute. But this response is not dead silence, nor a response of admiration, but of 'sustained attention.' "[24] The attainment of an attentive silence is one of the great achievements of art in a world that loudly persuades and endlessly coerces our senses.

One of the tests of an ecumenical education is the room it has for silence, stillness and nonverbal communication. In every religious tradition the last step before the divine is silence, a

23. Dewey, *Art as Experience*, pp. 105, 270 f.
24. Dwayne Huebner, "Curricular Language and Classroom Meanings," in *Language and Meaning*, ed. James McDonald and Robert Leeper (Washington, 1966), p. 24.

fact which poor talkative Christianity in the person of its preachers and teachers never seems to grasp. At its best, however, Christianity has turned to a form of art such as music to make contact with that realm "where all that is not music is silence." The music in ecumenical education need not be church music. However, the close relationship between religion and music all through history is not an accidental one. "With a force that no argument will ever equal, the music of Bach and Handel gives the conviction of crossing a frontier: such art is the irrefutable presence of an autonomous source of gracious and disinterested nobility, an absolute benignity of an order and spiritual authority about which nothing more perfect can ever be experienced or conceived. Though the reality of music is not God, it skirts his essence, as it were, and causes him to be perceived as a promised land whose existence can no longer be doubted."[25]

In order for life to make sense, indeed for life to survive at all, man needs to achieve a human and therefore aesthetic dimension in things. His cities, schools, churches and countryside disintegrate for lack of aesthetic understanding. Where *understanding* is the aim of education, rather than prediction or control, then only the dramatic mode suffices. Plato long ago realized that the dramatic is the highest form of education. For feelings to be shared in a way that does not threaten or coerce, we need modes of instruction that represent the human condition in drama. Through such drama we come to understand the drama of life itself.

Literature represents a further step into the realm of the rational and verbal while retaining contact with a more primitive experience of life. At this stage one encounters elements that are more directly and immediately religious, that is, there are pieces of literature that are the sacred books of a religion. By reading these works (Bhagavad Gita, Bible, Koran) one is

25. Maurice Nedoncelle, *Love and the Person* (New York, 1966), p. 232.

studying religion. However, none of these books is easy reading because of subject matter, style, date and place of origin. Masterpieces of religious literature should have an appropriate place in public education's study of literature. If such books, including the Christian bible, have much to tell us today, this fact ought to become apparent through a sensitive teacher and a comparison of good literature.

Before ever getting to religious literature, a young person is being ecumenically educated wherever words make a "raid on the inarticulate" (T. S. Eliot) and break open the world to something new. In this regard literature, like the other arts, is not so much a vehicle for religion as religion itself. Poetry is very close to prayer; it is very much a revelation, a conserver and a creator of the world. Wallace Stevens, speaking of religion and poetry, wrote: "Both have to mediate for us a reality not ourselves and . . . the supreme virtue here is humility, for the humble are they that move about the world with the lure of the real in their hearts."[26]

In speaking of the stories of childhood I pointed out that the immersion in fantasy and imagery is the foundation of any later quest in life. Although people may seem to accept this truth they usually turn to more "realistic" sources of information as they get older and dismiss all stories as childish. A strong tendency in this direction says a great deal about a society. "There is a certain embarrassment," Flannery O'Connor wrote, "about being a story teller in these times when stories are considered not quite as satisfying as statements and statements not quite as satisfying as statistics; but, in the long run, a people is known not by its statements or statistics, but by the stories it tells."[27]

The literature that has emerged in religious traditions runs the gamut of literary forms from epic to love poem. Religion

26. Quoted in Ray Hart, *Unfinished Man and the Imagination* (New York, 1968), pp. 310 f.
27. O'Connor, *op. cit.*, p. 192.

more than any other field has to have a feel for literature because it must try to express in words what is ultimately inexpressible. The debasement of language is the destruction of religion. Instead of wasting their efforts on keeping a few naughty words out of print, religious groups ought to be concerned with the imaginative and intelligible use of language. "The chief danger to philosophy of religion lies in the temptation to generalize what is essentially unique, to explicate what is intrinsically inexplicable, to adjust the uncommon to our common sense."[28]

A main failure of Christianity has been the disregarding of its own roots in language and literature. No one should be allowed to study theology, let alone write it, who has not "loved and been well nurtured in his mother tongue" (Keats). The dullness of theology books is a kind of sacrilege. In an era which bears some similarity to our own, Erasmus castigated the theologians of his day for failing to develop their skills by reading the classical poets, orators and historians. In a letter to Thomas More, he wrote: "The study of theology was solidly based on these now deposed expositors of fundamental truth during all the Christian centuries until the invention of these petty and meretricious *quaestiones* which alone today are tossed so glibly back and forth."[29]

A study of literature leads into the question of history. Here again, I am not primarily interested in the "sacred history" that religion books deal with. I am talking about the study of man, particularly the men of the past, that has a place in all education. There are numerous philosophical and methodological questions about history that I will not go into here. I wish simply to point out that unless some interest in history can be aroused, then the study of an "historical religion" is almost sure to be abortive. On the other hand, an appreciation of any history is

28. Abraham Heschel, *The Insecurity of Freedom* (New York, 1966), p. 119.
29. *Handbook of the Militant Christian* (Notre Dame, 1962), p. 39.

113

a step in the direction of a possible acceptance of Christian faith. The rise of the modern notion of history is traceable to rationality in Greco-Roman culture, attitudes in Judeo-Christian tradition and skills in the modern West. To study history is to enter the life of that civilization. The danger signal for that civilization, as Robert Lifton has pointed out, is the denial of the principle of historical continuity.[30]

It is this last attitude which seems to characterize so many young, and not so young, people today. Despite claims of religion books that history is what is central to modern man's awareness, there seems to be a wholesale revulsion against historical study. The rapidity of change in the contemporary world has led to a feeling that the past is irrelevant or even misleading. This kind of malaise is difficult to cope with but the sensitive men of today are warning us that it can only lead to catastrophe. Loren Eiseley writes: "To hurl oneself recklessly without method upon a future that we ourselves have complicated is a sheer nihilistic rejection of all that history, including the classical world, can teach us."[31] People who are trying to teach religion might consider whether the rejection of Moses and Jesus is not more a rejection of history than of religion.

In saner moments nearly everyone admits that the past should be known, if only to avoid repeating the mistakes of the past. A large part of the failure must lie in the way history is approached and the demands that are made upon it. If history were studied as the present life of man, and the past were constant background, there would probably be more interest in history. It may be asking too much of the word or the field to be stretched in that way. Perhaps it is a more candid and viable procedure to place the word experience at the center of education and then try to expand experience to take in the past. The study of man in the present would be the main subject of concern and the study of history would be in constant relation

30. Lifton, *op. cit.*, p. 362.
31. Eiseley, *op. cit.*, pp. 6 f.

to this focus. The purpose of teaching history in school might be shifted without undue violence to the scholarly discipline of history. In the curriculum that Jerome Bruner proposes, the core is anthropology and the behavioral sciences are central to the presentation. Bruner continues: "This is not to say that we should give up the study of the past, but rather that we should pursue such study with a different end in view—the end of developing style. For the development of style, be it style of writing or loving or dancing or eating, requires a sense of contrast and concreteness, and this we do not find in the behavioral sciences."[32]

The sciences represent the epitome of man's rationality and his most precise encounter with reality. In studying science a young person meets one of the indirect effects of Christian faith and at the same time one of the great challenges that must be met if Christianity is to make any sense today. The study of the natural sciences, therefore, belongs to an ecumenical education, not because there is a Christian chemistry but because the unleashing of man's power of critical reason should be a chief concern of Christianity. "Science was born and has grown out of the conviction that faithful enquiry can release mankind from bondage to ignorance, superstition and prejudice."[33]

It should not be surprising that this discovery ignites a reaction, and usually an overreaction, to the ignorance, myths, superstition and stories of childhood. What science did historically should probably be expected in an individual life, namely, it depopulates the heavens and de-myths the earth. Recent Christian theology insists that this process is normal and good, that Christianity is partial cause and ultimate benefactor of the process. Instead of trying to prop up childish religious beliefs, the church representative should perhaps rejoice at the "secularization" of the young student of science.

32. Bruner, *Toward a Theory of Instruction*, pp. 36 f.
33. Philip Phenix, "Liberal Learning and the Practice of Freedom," in *Christian Scholar*, 50 (Spring, 1967), p. 11.

The rejoicing, however, should not be without qualification. The scientization process should not be so complete that it loses touch with the poetic world that precedes it and the humanized universe that ought to receive it. We do not need less science in our education but we do need more humanistic study that will provide a context for the crowning achievement of reason.

The way in which science is taught is influential in determining whether science becomes deified so that it attains its own priesthood, ideology and magic, or whether it is a step toward a mature but always tentative understanding of the universe. It has been found that for the sake of science itself, the theories of science cannot be propagated as the final revelation of how the universe really is. The changes occurring today in the teaching of science should be of more than passing interest to those concerned with religious education. "The new theories of the scientists are likewise poetic statements which partake of this joy of creation. Unfortunately, the expressive statements of young children are too frequently ignored or pushed into the venerable coin of the realm by tired adult questions or conditioned responses, and science is taught as a body of knowns and sure things rather than as an activity of man which illuminates the unknown and man's poetic character."[34]

The study of the *human* sciences is a further understanding of man's place in the world. This study is more obviously connected to ecumenical education than the study of natural science because of its unavoidable concern with human values. There is more and more admission today that the great questions of politics, society and economics cannot be met without raising questions of human values. Churches cannot and should not try to dictate the values that are expounded. In fact, no one should simply "dictate" them but many people should be concerned that the issues are openly discussed in a nonthreatening and nonpunitive environment. Schools that fail to raise these

34. Huebner, *loc. cit.*, p. 21.

challenges of value cannot be providing much of an education.[35]

It has been a common belief in Christian tradition, and probably still is, that morality cannot be discussed without bringing in religion. That the moral foundation of society would disintegrate without religion is a thesis which could be plausibly argued. It seems certain, nonetheless, that many people today are acutely aware of moral or human values who will have nothing to do with religion. It is likewise a fact that it is possible to talk in school about human values and moral choices while avoiding nearly all the religious disputes. Many religionists may think that this possibility is not worth striving for or even that it is dangerous. I would claim that the consideration of human values outside of religious discussion is both possible and desirable. Particularly for Christianity, which supposedly caps human development but so often short-circuits the process, it is important that human values arise from human contexts.

Only after all of these paths of art, literature, history and science have been followed out does there arise the possibility and the need for a study of religion. It should be noted that religion will already have been directly encountered in the study of history and of literature, it will have been met more obliquely in the arts and sciences. With such a backdrop, religion can then be examined as a phenomenon in itself that can be understood from within. Thus, I have placed the study of religion on a comparative basis at the conclusion of these other studies and at the beginning of an ecumenical synthesis.

A survey or summary of individual religious traditions cannot be set out here. However, I wish to stress the importance of the principle of comparativeness. Many young people who are taught the Christian religion will not accept it today. It is not so much that they reject it as they cannot understand it without comparing it to alternatives. There is a widespread demand

35. See William Glasser, *Schools Without Failure* (New York, 1969), p. 192; Viktor Frankl, *The Will to Meaning* (New York, 1969), p. 46; Kenneth Boulding, *Beyond Economics* (Ann Arbor, 1968), p. 194.

for courses in religions other than Christianity. This demand is a simple and legitimate one springing from the desire to know, understand and appreciate other religious options before excluding them.

The Supreme Court of the United States, in clarifying its position after the famous school prayer decision, pointed out that the study of religion was not forbidden in public education. In fact, the Court indicated that such study was desirable. It did stipulate, however, that only an "objective" teaching of religion was acceptable.[36] The word objective may have been a poor choice in this context insofar as it is highly ambiguous. Religionists are quick to point out that subjective involvement is part of faith and that to teach religion from a neutral position is to do violence to it. As one critic has put it: "Academic treatment of God will not lead to acceptance of Him as the divine. On the contrary, there is good reason to expect it will set off an opposing tendency. Such courses are useful, interesting, and academically respectable, but they serve another purpose. They do not make men religious."[37]

To deal with this argument one would have to investigate what meaning a writer gives to the word religion. It is undeniable that the study of religion does not make men religious in the sense of uncritical attachment to the tradition they were brought up in. The study of religion does contribute to the breakdown of primitive religiosity although sometimes it may be more a result than a cause. "The study of religion thrives best when religious life falters. When the church and synagogue are weak, then religious study will be strong because people will be questioning and thinking about their traditional religious roots."[38]

36. See Claire Cox, *The Fourth R* (New York, 1969), pp. 13–28; James Pannoch and David Barr, *Religion Goes to School* (New York, 1968), p. 55.

37. Stoops, *op. cit.*, p. 34.

38. Robert Spivey, "Modest Messiahs: The Study of Religion in State Universities," in *Religious Education*, 63 (Jan./Feb., 1968), pp. 5–12.

The meaning of the word objective can be clarified by opposing it to two words, noninvolved and nonimpartial. The academic treatment of religion should be objective in the sense that it is impartial. When the word objective is used with a positive connotation, the values attached to the word are fairness, accuracy, and lack of arbitrariness. An objective treatment points not to a negation of subjective involvement but to impartiality. A person can have convictions and still decide a case impartially, that is, he respects evidence and judges with integrity.

It is not just in public education that religion should be so examined. Whenever religion is educationally at issue it ought to be taught in an intellectually respectable and non-proselytizing manner. Such religion of itself probably never converted anyone to a church or religion, but that is not the reason for having courses. The reason for studying religion is to understand it so that when one does choose to live by it or not to live by it, his choice will be an intelligent one. Neither the Court nor common sense would exclude Catholics from teaching about Catholicism or Jews from teaching Judaism. Presumably those people could do it best who know their own tradition from the inside out. Passionate involvement and strong conviction do not preclude the kind of objectivity that intellectual integrity requires.

Whether the direct study of religion can be begun in the pre-adult phase of ecumenical education is questionable. Certainly, this kind of study can take place at the university level in a course on comparative religion. Perhaps a course of this kind can begin in the upper years of secondary school. With Catholic high school students today it is difficult to determine what kind of religion study might be possible because they are usually in revolt against the oversaturation of religion that they have already received. Even good religion programs for senior high school students have to spend most of their energies in trying

119

to overcome the credibility gap which earlier teaching has produced.

The path to the study of Christianity which I have outlined in this chapter may seem long and circuitous. Many people would prefer a quick and easy route. "There are many people," wrote Kierkegaard, "who reach their conclusions about life like schoolboys. They cheat their master by copying the answer out of a book without having worked out the sum for themselves."[39] Many committed Christians would like to save their children the pain of looking for religious answers. In the long run such help is not to the service of the person growing up. In our world today the survival of Christianity rests on having people who freely belong because they understand what they are doing and have faced the real possibility of choosing otherwise.

39. Søren Kierkegaard, *The Journals of Kierkegaard* (New York, 1958), p. 53.

6. Adult Religious Education

THE first premise of this book is that the field of religious education must be reborn out of a coalition of good education and sound theology. The second premise is that theology and education both point to the centrality of experience for all religious education. The third premise is that if experience were actually central to religious education, then the field would have to be developed from the perspective of adult centeredness. My conviction is that we have yet to reach the first of these three premises so that the apparent concern with experience and adults in religious education is mostly illusory. An "experience centered" course may be offered in a Catholic school and then be abandoned as unworkable. A CCD may try adult education as its pitch for a year or two and then conclude that adults are not interested.

In the title of this chapter I have placed the word adult first as a modifier of religious education. I am talking less about adult education courses than a religious education that has an adult character. Throughout this book I talk about religious education that is directed toward an adult mentality and is defined by reference to some adult model. This is a religious education that is offered in an adult way for people who wish to become more adult. In this context, a course that genuinely respects the person and intelligently criticizes the opinions of 13-year-olds may be very much directed to adulthood. In contrast, a course for 43-year-olds in which a lecturer delivers half-baked ideas to his listeners may be a very childish course. We urgently need education by adults for adults to become more adult. As the third use of the word reveals, we have to distinguish between the chronological meaning of adulthood and adulthood in a psychic, social and religious sense. This chapter will be mainly concerned with exploring the ideal of the mature adult and the relation of religious faith to this ideal.

Before moving into that question, I would like to comment on the concept of adult education. I have claimed that what we need is lifelong education. The expansion of the number of years that a child is kept in school may seem to be a move toward lifelong education. Actually this tendency runs counter to the movement for lifelong education because it misconceives the relation between schooling and experience. Education that is lifelong would understand the school to be a clarifying of experience so that schools would be for everyone part of the time and for no one all of the time.

This question of the relation between school and experience must be raised whenever there is discussion of adult education, or, as it is revealingly called, "continuing education." If continuing education conceives of itself simply as continuing the same old thing as the children get, it should not be surprised when it is not a striking success. I said earlier that the addition of adult education courses, in isolation from any other change in education, would be less a help than a hindrance to the development of an adult centered education. I am by no means opposing the growth of adult education. In fact, I am claiming that it ought to start thinking of itself as the dog rather than the tail. Books on adult education, despite some brave claims to importance, are often afflicted with inferiority complexes. The problem is not helped by the murky style that seems to characterize books in this area.

The reason for the inferiority complex is easy to come by: in practice adult education is inferior. Generally speaking, at least, adult education courses are not well backed, well taught or well administered. Apparently it is difficult for many people to believe that adult education is serious educational business. After describing adult education as the fastest growing part of education, Peter Drucker makes the comment that "the academic community is still somewhat suspicious of anyone past adolescence who wants to learn."[1] Education being a commodity that is given to children, it must be presumed that there is something a little queer about people who are interested in learning later in life. It has been said of the New School for Social Research that it grew upside down because it began with continuing education and subsequently developed a graduate school and an undergraduate college.[2] It would be considered flippant to suggest that perhaps it is the rest of education, and not the New School, that grew upside down. The conviction is still firm and unyielding: schools are for children and, more depressingly, children are for schools.

My suggestions for adult religious education come from what I believe is the future of general adult education. For the present, of course, the adult religious education that I am advocating does have a fairly secure foothold in the university. Both church related colleges and public universities can offer, and many are offering, adult religious education, that is, a study in ecumenical religion/Christianity. The university, however, is not an all-sufficient instrument to cope with this educational problem. More formal education is needed for adults in our society whether these forms derive from existing universities, continuing education centers, or other avenues yet to be discovered.

Any proposals to shift religious education in the direction of adults may seem hopelessly utopian and institutionally naive. One must admit the utopian character but with the added thought of Oscar Wilde that "a map of the world that does not include Utopia is not worth glancing at for it leaves out the one country at which Humanity is always landing." The fact that utopia cannot be reached immediately does not preclude

1. Drucker, *op. cit.,* p. 321.
2. See J. Kirk Sale, "The New School at Middle Age," in *Change,* 1 (July-Aug., 1969), pp. 37–45.

123

its gradually shaping our attitudes and eventually changing our institutions. Lifelong religious education is never going to be much better than the institutions available for general education. However, in this instance I am suggesting that religious education could take a role of leadership rather than be in the rear guard. Some of the experiences and resources of the church could be used in the service of making all education adult centered. The church could not complete the job of reorienting education but it could make a significant contribution to it. In any case, those people who are taking up the cry for adult education in the churches ought to be forewarned that the structures for their work are weak, if existent at all. They had better not start at all unless they are willing to build for the long term future. Far from discouraging anyone, these facts should lead to a redoubling of effort by all parties interested in the church's role in education.

In regard to existing adult or continuing education, whatever its nascent condition, there are several facts that should be of interest for people in religious education. First, the most obvious cause for the rise of adult education is the growing complexity of the technological order. Before World War II adult education was aimed at the poorly educated, giving the bright but poor the chance they did not have as children. This picture, however, has changed dramatically over the past twenty-five years. The accelerated rate of technological change began to create a demand for retraining in certain professional skills. This tendency has been broadening to include the whole population which must constantly readapt itself for life in the new order. Although only perhaps one-fourth of the population actually takes part in some formal adult education, it is on the way to becoming a necessity for everyone. "First, it is no longer the case that continued learning through adult life is a necessity only for the minority of professional scholars. It is now a necessity in the life of everyone who would not be a mere slave in the society he serves. Second, no longer can casual information processes of learning enable an adult to change his thought and action in response to the changes occurring around him. Not only is change too rapid for this gradual process; it is also too deep and penetrates too many aspects of life to permit an adequate adjustment by untutored trial and error."[3]

Instead of being remedial for the poorly educated, adult education today appeals to those who have more education. The better educated a person is, the more likely he is to wish to continue learning.[4] It is also true, however, at least in the early part of adult life, that the main interest is in occupational training: engineers learning to be better engineers, pilots of prop planes learning to fly jets, surgeons learning new operations. Only about one-fourth of adult education concerns public affairs and the humanities. However, it is of considerable interest for religious education that the relative interest in general educational concerns, as opposed to occupational concerns, increases with age. After people have attained competence in their work or have shifted to new work in middle age, they may begin to raise human questions that include the philosophical and religious.[5] This fact is encouraging when combined with other evidence that the adult's learning ability continues to grow during life. Although learning ability may decrease if not used and may be affected by physical impairment, the capacity to grow in understanding never stops.[6] There is no reason why an older adult cannot be a most avid student of religion.

Technology supplies the biggest pressure for adult training and this training is mainly occupational or technical. Somewhat paradoxically, however, technology is forcing to the front education for non-job activities. Technology not only creates more

3. Kimball and McClellan, *op. cit.,* p. 295.

4. See Malcolm Knowles, "Adult Education," in *The New Media and Education,* ed. Peter Rossi and Bruce Biddle (Garden City, 1967), pp. 337 ff.

5. See Alan Knox, *The Audience for Liberal Adult Education* (Chicago, 1962).

6. See Douglas Sjogren and Alan Knox, *The Influence of Speed, Attitude and Prior Knowledge on Adult Learning* (Lincoln, Neb., 1965).

complicated jobs, it does away with some jobs and reduces the time needed in other jobs. When technology reduced the work week from 72 to 60 hours there was little problem in using the extra 12 hours to relax. But should the work week be reduced to 25 hours or 12 hours there will then be an acute problem of "killing time." New forms of human activity are already needed to deal with the "problem of leisure." Perhaps the original connection between the words leisure and school can be rediscovered. This hope may seem unrealistic in face of the almost universal tendency to equate leisure and nonactivity. There is a limit to this tendency, however, because eventually human beings have to find something to *do*. "At that point," Michael Harrington has written, "it will be necessary to regard activities which have been thought of as hobbies, pleasures and avocations as the serious business of the society. Then the arts and sports and even philosophy will take on a new meaning. For now, it is possible . . . to begin to redefine what intelligence is."[7]

The arts, humanities and religion cannot compete with occupational courses for immediate and lucrative gain. Nonetheless, if it comes to a choice between money and self-dignity, the latter may loom more and more important in an age of intelligent machines. At the least it should be recognized that getting a man a job may be an important part of helping the disadvantaged but not the only part. Job training may be the most urgent adult educational need but in the long run it will only be successful if it is part of a larger program of education. As people move from one profession to a second, leave one *ad hoc* team for another, work within the family and beyond it, they will need a variety of humanistic forms of education to preserve a sense of self worth and fidelity to others. They may find the need to drop out of a job and into school for six months or a year in the new and fluid life cycle. With an optimistic view in this direction, Thomas Green writes: "As we move forward to a

7. Michael Harrington, *Toward a Democratic Left* (New York, 1968), p. 162.

leisure society, there is every reason to expect adult education—as it is focused both toward specific jobs and toward public affairs and the arts—to find its place among the leaders in educational growth. And we would therefore expect the agencies of education, including business, industries and divisions of local federal government, to multiply and to become more diverse in their aims and interests. This is precisely what is in fact happening."[8]

Education must be directed, therefore, toward the living of a mature, adult human life. At this point I would like to comment on the adult model that is presupposed here. To a large extent I am simply restating the anthropological picture of chapter three with particular emphasis on the word adult. The ideal of childhood and the ideal of youth can hardly be understood unless they are related to an adult model. Strangely enough, there has been less attention given to the psychology of the adult than to that of children and youth, but perhaps this is soon to change. Erik Erikson has recently written. "As we have already passed the 'century of the child' and are now experiencing, with a vengeance, that of the adolescent, we may well be entering a period in which we must dare to ask: 'What, really, is an adult?' "[9]

There is, of course, a great deal implicit in modern psychology and other sciences to answer the question, "what really is an adult?" Despite differences among schools of thought in the study of man, one can highlight a few points on which there is remarkable agreement.[10] It is possible to state some characteristics of an adult life as opposed to characteristics of a childish outlook. The use of the word adult in this context presupposes a value judgment about proper growth and development. When Kenneth Keniston writes that "only an adult can be a 'pro-

8. Green, *op. cit.*, p. 101.

9. Erik Erikson, "Reflections on the Dissent of Contemporary Youth," in *Daedalus*, 99 (Winter, 1970), p. 175.

10. See Douglas Heath, *Explorations of Maturity* (New York, 1965), pp. 3–35.

fessional youth,' " he is referring to someone who in terms of years is an adult but who is living a style of life that, judged by certain criteria, is proper to youth. One might argue about the criteria for such a judgment but the point remains that it is possible to speak about childish adults, adolescent adults and adult adults. Whether the adult adult does not in fact retain or assimilate some of the qualities of children and youth is a matter for investigation. For the moment, I wish only to emphasize that my present use of the word adult refers to people who, adult in years, are living adult lives (by criteria of personal development).

In Chapter 2 of this book and in previous writings I have claimed that the psycho-social model of maturity converges with the faith model of Judaic-Christian tradition. The evidence for this claim is not obviously conclusive. At the least, however, it can be maintained that both Judaism and Christianity were fundamentally opposed to a magical and childish attitude toward the universe.[11] The failure of Christianity to carry through its own inherent drive is also fairly evident. But the Christian model of life, namely, to grow up into the freedom and fullness of Christ, remains central to Christian faith.

One important qualification must be added to the statement that there is a convergence of the Judaic-Christian model of faith and the psycho-social model of adulthood. The word convergence is carefully chosen in this statement. Christianity must be aware of what constitutes human wholeness or health and be constantly trying to incorporate this data. Anything which contributes to the adult development of man ought to be approved and supported by Christian believers. On the other hand, one must not move from approving what is adult to condemning what is not adult. Some people will never reach adulthood. Far from condemning such people Christianity is supposed to be particularly attentive to them, both to give help to them and to learn some-

11. See Max Weber, *On Charisma and Institutional Building* (Chicago, 1968), p. 158.

thing from them. One of the ways of revising and improving the model of adulthood is to have it challenged by those who can never fit it. In an article entitled "Mental Retardation: The Cry of Why?" Carl J. Rote writes: "The retardates have taught me more than I can ever tell. Theirs is a world where hypocrisy is banished; it is a kingdom where a smile is their passport to your affection and the light in their eyes will melt the coldest heart. Perhaps this is God's way of reminding us that the world must rediscover the attributes which the mentally retarded have never lost."[12]

It is incorrect to assume that holiness and health are the same thing even though we may say that the two converge. It is false to say that to be an adult is to be a Christian or to be a Christian is to be an adult. The first is said by some people who wish to claim too much and who do violence to language and credibility by designating people (anonymously) Christian. The second is grossly erroneous if it excludes from Christianity the psychologically maimed, mentally retarded and prophetically unbalanced who prick our neat assumptions about full manhood. A few years ago an article of mine was given the title: "Christianity: A Religion for Adults," a phrase that became something of a slogan. At best it is a misleading slogan and at worst it badly distorts the particular concern which Christianity should have for the non-adults.

The problem I am trying to clarify here is not caused by a confusion over the word adult. If that were the problem, it could be eliminated by a few definitions. Actually, the problem is at the heart of Christianity and religion itself. Judaism and Christianity did not add a final touch to what men would quite reasonably think of life. This tradition (and other great religious traditions) supported all of humanity by the paradoxical route of challenging man's highest powers of reasoning. Religion brings into operation another kind of truth from the seer, the mystic, the ascetic, the maimed, the dispossessed and the fanatic.

12. Quoted in Frankl, *op. cit.*, p. 140.

This religious challenge prevents man from making any final judgments about the fullness of manhood. It keeps permanently open the perfecting of mankind. If the last judgment on man were man's, we would indeed be miserable men. In his beautiful book, *Images of Hope,* William Lynch writes: "I would point out to the medical man that there is a Christian legend of the wicked angels who fell from heaven because they were given an anticipatory vision of the humanity of Christ and refused to adore it. It occurs to me that the medical men are daily asked to watch an analogous situation as they observe the gnostic part in all of us refusing even elementary acceptance of our own humanity."[13]

To be a Christian, therefore, is to be moving toward the complete adulthood we never reach. A retarded child, on his own terms, may be moving faster and better in that direction than a theology professor. The insistence in this book on the educational preparation needed for Christianity presumes that most people are going to be exposed to the kind of education that has evolved in this country. Those who are outside the mainstream are not excluded from being Christians. They may find another and an even better route. The great problem is not people with a third grade educational level who are at the same level of religious education. The people that have the worst problem are those who have Ph.D's in engineering but a high school religious education. The gap between the two of them rather than the total amount of religious education, creates the difficulties. Some people who have never received any religious education may be the greatest saints Christianity has. This fact does not excuse us, who for better or worse have been exposed to education, from trying to devise models, ideals and objectives for an educated adult.

There are many different ways that one could proceed in trying to describe an adult attitude. One could begin by saying that to become adult is to become free. The statement is correct but we should realize that citing freedom as the adult characteristic

13. William Lynch, *Images of Hope* (New York, 1966), p. 188.

is more a restating of the question than it is an answering of the question. Although it is often used today, a typology of free and unfree is not very helpful for describing the human race unless these two categories can be filled in.

A start toward elaborating the meaning of freedom can be made by recalling from Chapter 3 the connection between freedom and the availability of experience. Both Maslow and Rogers stress the need to eliminate obstacles that block out self-perception. There has to be some "congruence" between the self-image and the experience of the organism. The availability of experience to consciousness does not necessarily imply a very reflective self-consciousness. When there is a possibility of facing, understanding and symbolically expressing experience, a person can relax, act spontaneously, and simply *be* himself.[14] Behavior can then be directed to coping with problems rather than defending against them. No one can block out awareness of all experience nor does anyone perfectly assimilate experience but there are degrees in the obstruction of experience which can be used to measure freedom.

This negatively defined freedom leads easily into a description of some of the qualities which every mature person should have. Gordon Allport reduced these to three main characteristics: "First, a variety of psychogenic interests is required which concern themselves with ideal objects and values beyond the range of viscerogenic desire . . . A second attribute is the ability to objectify oneself, to be reflective and insightful about one's own life . . . Finally, a mature personality always has some unifying philosophy of life, although not necessarily religious in type, nor articulated in words, nor entirely complete."[15]

In this description of the mature person, Allport indicates that

14. See Lawrence Kubie, "The Forgotten Man of Education," in *Contemporary Educational Psychology*, ed. Richard Jones (New York, 1967), pp. 65 f.; also Rogers, *On Becoming a Person*, p. 359; Maslow, *Psychology of Science*, pp. 36 f.
15. Gordon Allport, *The Individual and His Religion* (New York, 1960), p. 53.

131

a great diversity of life (no. 1) and a strong unity to life (no. 3) are held in fruitful tension by a deep understanding of one's place in life (no. 2). This division is helpful for seeing what the problem of freedom is and also why there is constant misunderstanding of it. Adulthood itself involves the refusal to drive for a final and total solution to the problem of freedom.

In Everett Shostrom's fine little book, *Man the Manipulator,* he contrasts two types that he calls the actualizor and the manipulator; the former is becoming more free but the latter, because he thinks he has solved the problem of freedom, lives by manipulating himself and others. Shostrom writes: "Here I must make what is perhaps the most important statement of this book: while the manipulator is a many faceted person of antagonistic opposites, the actualizor is a many faceted person of complementary opposites."[16] Several important points are contained in this short statement: first, no one is either simple or complex but everyone is a complex bundle; second, differences among people spring from their differing awareness and acceptance of the several sides of their personality; third, the integrity we yearn for can only be found and must only be sought for as a delicately balanced tension of opposites. "The value of the structure which is finally achieved will be proportionate to the strength of the tension between the combined opposites and the number of the polar forces which enter into the new combination."[17] Strong contrasting forces that can live in relative peace within the unity of an organismic system is practically a definition of adult life.

The assumption is widespread that adult means being rational rather than irrational, controlled rather than spontaneous, independent rather than dependent. According to how each of those words is defined it may be true that adulthood should have

16. Everett Shostrom, *Man the Manipulator* (New York, 1968), p. 26.
17. Neuman, *Depth Psychology and the New Ethic,* p. 101; Slater, *op. cit.,* pp. 110 f.

a high degree of rationality, control and independence. But one must be careful of trying to get a desirable quality by obliterating what seems to be the opposite. What apparently is opposite to a desirable quality may be a necessary dimension of human life and thus cannot be simply eliminated. For example, Erik Erikson's well known description of the developmental tasks in the life cycle (trust vs. mistrust, autonomy vs. doubt, initiative vs. guilt, industry vs. inferiority, identity vs. role diffusion, intimacy vs. isolation, generativity vs. self-absorption and integrity vs. despair) must not be used as a scorecard so that the first term of each pair is to exclude the second. While Erikson undoubtedly thinks that trust is better than distrust and generativity is better than self-absorption, he also knows that life is partly hoping and partly despairing, loving and hating, trusting and not trusting. The conflict of A and B in human personality is not resolved by the victory of A or B but by the attainment of C which provides a *modus vivendi* for A and B.

Two examples, rationality and independence, will serve to clarify the above principle. An adult is a person who has come to terms with the rational and the nonrational elements of his self. He has not identified himself with one or the other nor has he left himself in two pieces between which he veers erratically. He is always in the process of integrating the two; indeed, he knows himself *to be* the process. Such a person has a gentle rhythm to his life, bringing to bear at one moment the clear light of reason and at another moment letting go of his rational control to make other contact with life. There is a vast difference between not having rational control and being able to relinquish it when desirable. "The difference is the same as the one between the person who can *visit* the slums and the one who is forced to live there always. (Either world is a slum if one can't leave it.) Then, paradoxically, that which was sick and pathological and the 'lowest' becomes part of the healthiest and 'highest' aspects of human nature. Slipping into 'craziness' is frightening only

133

for those who are not fully confident of their sanity. Education must help the person to live in both worlds."[18]

A similar process of combination pertains to independence. Freedom is often thought to be identical with independence or not being dependent upon others. The manipulator makes this identification and then has to concentrate on getting control of others (and part of himself) inasmuch as he cannot avoid interaction of some kind. Adult freedom consists in the recognition and acceptance of the fact that dependence is one side to life and that it cannot be avoided. In fact, the richness of life springs from this dependence. The question is not whether to be dependent or independent but *how* to be both. The answer resides in finding a way to be dependently independent and independently dependent. A child has needs and is satisfied through his dependence on those who satisfy his needs. An adult, besides the residual needs from childhood which he should now satisfy for himself, has a new and different kind of need. The peculiarly adult need is the need to be needed. Because this need is personal, and of its nature mutual and reciprocal, then the dependency of an adult does not have to decrease his selfhood. When adults satisfy the adult needs of others there is no loss to anyone. The mutual surrender of human selves increases the richness, freedom and independence of both.

The greatest danger to adulthood is the reduction of this rich, variegated, paradoxical world to a monodimensional list of qualities. The human being is so adept at self-deception that anyone who tries to give a description of adult freedom is likely to prejudice it in his own favor. It can be said, nonetheless, that as a person moves toward adulthood his behavior becomes more difficult to predict but more dependable and appropriate. The steadiness of his character is not the dull sameness of logical consistency but a kaleidoscope of human possibilities held together without external pressure. With commitment that includes detachment, passion that has order, and creativity that

18. Maslow, *Psychology of Science,* pp. 198 f.

springs from what is given, an adult has found a way to live with freedom and grow into it more each day. At the end, freedom, Emmanuel Mounier wrote, "is relaxation, receptiveness, preparedness, availability, and ultimately association. The free man is the man to whom the world puts questions and who responds accordingly."

One corollary to this adult attitude which has been implied throughout the previous description concerns a person's attitude toward time. To be always in the midst of achieving a synthesis of opposites and to be living in a gentle rhythm between poles of experience is equivalent to living in the present. To accept one's experience is to be aware of what is going on now. "Most of us," writes Rogers, "bring a preformed structure and never relinquish it, but cram and twist the experience to fit our preconceptions, annoyed at the fluid qualities which make it so unruly in fitting our carefully constructed pigeon-holes. To open one's spirit to what is going on *now*, and to discover in that present process whatever structure it appears to have—this to me is one of the qualities of the good life, the mature life, as I see clients approach it."[19]

It sounds like a balanced and unchallengeable position to say that we should integrate past, present and future. Warnings not to overemphasize the present usually follow such statements. However, this apparent solution fails to grasp the nature of the problem of time and does not understand the particular character of the present. The present is not a segment of time comparable to the past and future but the way in which past and future intersect in human relationships. It is impossible to live too much in the present and to overemphasize the present. To treat the present as if it were a segment of time obscures the problem man has with nature and his own bodiliness.

To be free is to remember the past and anticipate the future but to live in the present. The living between the tension of past and future is one more application of the law of unity in con-

19. Rogers, *On Becoming a Person*, p. 189.

trast. Contrary to what is usually assumed, there is very little difference between trying to live in the past or in the future. Both are an escape from experience and a violation of nature. Escape and violation eventually take their toll. "Many adults feel that their worth as people consists entirely in what they are 'going at' in the future and not in what they are in the present. The strain consequently developed in their bodies, which are always 'on the go' with the engine racing even at moments of rest, is a powerful contribution to the much discussed psychosomatic diseases of our time."[20]

Time is neither linear nor circular for man; it is an attitude, an interiority and a relation that has linear and cyclical movement to it plus much else. To be human is to be willing to wait for appointed moments which are ever new but not entirely new. The capacity to live through human time is manifest in celebration which is the living out "in an uncommon manner the universal assent to the world."[21] At one level this attitude appears to be that of a child's. On a more profound level, adulthood is the recognition of receptiveness, presence and celebration not as the toys of the child but as the truth of the human. Life is more complicated than childhood knows but life is also as simple as childhood seems to assume. To be an adult is to know both of these truths and knowing them to live by them.

It remains to comment more explicitly on the role of ecumenical faith and on the study of faith for an adult. In a passage quoted above, Gordon Allport gives as one of the criteria of maturity a unified philosophy of life. This coherent outlook may be attainable without religious faith but religion at its best has traditionally played that role. Adulthood entails the realization that a person is not the center of the world but only an uncompleted fragment of the world. This experience of smallness and incompleteness could be the beginning of frustration and despair unless there is a faith which allows one to resituate his per-

20. Erik Erikson, *Identity: Youth and Crisis* (New York, 1968), p. 120.
21. Pieper, *op. cit.*, p. 23.

spective. "What if the focus of his concern were shifted? Might not becoming a part of a larger, more significant whole relieve his life of its oppressive triviality? This question, once it arises, brings the beginning of religion. For though in some watered down sense there may be a religion which makes of the self its own god, true religion begins with the quest for meaning and value beyond privacy—with renunciation of the ego's claim to finality."[22]

Man seems destined to one of two paths: either to retreat into himself to preserve some semblance of stability or else to set out on the perilous journey of looking for a true self by letting go of the self he possesses. The latter alternative cannot be undertaken without profound belief in the trustworthiness of the universe. The belief may remain implicit and never be articulated but it must be there, nonetheless. Only in a world where the most fundamental dynamism of things is good does it make sense to seek a better world. This trust in wholeness may be expressed in a variety of ways: an Einstein who believed that the gods do not play dice with the universe, the Hindu search for the path of wisdom in which the truth of Brahman-Atman is revealed, or the Christian following of Christ to the heavenly Father. All belief cannot be reduced to some lowest common denominator but there is a common element which runs throughout lives profoundly human and which keeps men from going mad. This faith changes from age to age, culture to culture, person to person and the difference in expression is far from insignificant. The fact remains, nevertheless, that a religious or quasi-religious faith, that is, an unprovable assumption about the experienced universe, is what holds together the opposites in adult life.

The widespread claim that modern man has so fundamentally changed that he no longer needs belief must therefore be challenged. That he finds the rites of his religion alien, its doctrines unintelligible, its ethic irrelevant, may all be true. For such a

22. Huston Smith, *The Religions of Man* (New York, 1958), p. 22.

man the world is indeed empty of god. He may see no other alternative than to banish from consideration all religious matters and get on with the serious business of perfecting the earth. And yet he cannot solve the underlying dilemma of the universe which gave rise to religion in the first place. With a strange kind of logic he will of necessity fill in the vacuum caused by the demise of his religion. Peter Berger reports the somewhat amusing statistic that in a recent German poll it was found that 68% of people expressed belief in God while 86% admitted to praying.[23] In the need for belief modern man may be more like his forebears than he cares to admit.

Nowhere so much as in the matter of death does the question of faith loom so large. Religions grew up in large part as a counteraction to death, that is, as a way of giving some kind of meaning to what is apparently absurd and as a way of holding together society in face of the terror of chaos.[24] Religion, in recent times, has been criticized for promising pie in the sky and for diverting men's attention away from the earth. Since Marx, "to sin against the earth is the greatest sin." For modern man to keep his efforts directed at earth's task, it has seemed necessary to declare that death is a minor event to be accepted along with other slight inconveniences of modern life. Whatever was frightening about it has been hidden as much as possible except for those times when one is allowed to view it from the safe distance of a spectator.

The strategy has not been entirely successful. Even more than nature, death keeps sneaking back. Neither theories nor funeral parlors succeed in eliminating this central and stark reality of human life. The quest for some symbolic immortality continues, if not in overtly religious ways, then in nature, in youth or in new experiments. Robert Lifton describes the quest of "protean man" for immortality in "experimental 'transcendence'—of

23. Berger, *Rumor of Angels*, p. 30 f.
24. See Peter Berger and Thomas Luckmann, *The Social Construction of Reality* (Garden City, 1967), p. 101; also Bronislaw Malinowski, *Magic, Science and Religion* (Garden City, 1954), pp. 47–53.

seeking a sense of immortality in the way that mystics always have, through psychic experience of such great intensity that time and earth are, in effect, eliminated. This, I believe, is the larger meaning of the 'drug revolution,' of protean man's hunger for chemical aids to 'expand consciousness.' And indeed, all revolutions may be thought of, at bottom, as innovations in the struggle for immortality, as new combinations of old modes."[25]

Recent Christian theology has tried to avoid dealing directly with death. The desire was correctly based upon the belief that religions, including Christianity, had unfairly seized upon death as a weapon to subdue men into faith. The error, however, was not the concern with death but the inorganic nature of the concern which ripped death out of its context as a human event of human life. Instinctive terror and numbing fear are not the basis of a humanly integrating faith. Neither is the avoidance of the most profound human anxiety the path to integrity.

I have repeatedly said that there is a pre-rational and childish way to approach human problems and there is also a supra-rational and adult way to deal with the same problems. A society that takes adolescence as its ideal is likely to equate these two contrasting attitudes. There is a childish concern with death that leads to flight and magic. There is also a concern with death that is proper to adulthood in which a person has come to terms with the ambiguities of experience, the finitude of life and the inevitability of death. We need, as Sam Keen has suggested, courses on dying.[26] It is a concern particularly appropriate for Christian theology to handle. In fact, the supposition of this book is that it is only when death becomes a real expectation within one's experience that Christian theology can be taught at all. For the vast number of children who study religion, the death/resurrection theme of Christianity or other religions can only be so much verbiage.

25. Lifton, *op. cit.*, p. 330; see also Mircea Eliade, *The Quest: History and Meaning in Religion* (Chicago, 1969), p. 98.
26. Sam Keen, *To a Dancing God* (New York, 1970), pp. 74–80.

Even for young adults, many of whom do face death, the expectation of the end of life is still somewhat foreign to their experience. At such periods of life Christianity can only be a silent partner, or at most it can be conveyed in indirect ways. "There is good reason to suppose," wrote Gordon Allport, "that on the average the early and middle twenties are, in fact, the least religious period of life. It is then that the alienation from parental codes has become complete. It is then also that youth feels most secure in pursuing his life ambition. He has not yet had the rude shock that comes to nearly all adults when they first realize that their abilities and probable accomplishments are, after all, not likely to equal their aims and pretensions."[27] Some modification of this statement would probably be needed today. Religion in both traditional and bizarre forms seems to have been making headway with this age group. Courses dealing with religious alternatives should be available in the university. It is still probably true, however, that the majority of students will not be excited by the subject.

I would insist that the theological concern with death is not morbid, life-denying, or attacking men in their weakest spot. As Carl Ogletree notes: "We are scarcely 'spying out' men's weaknesses when we condemn the inhuman consequences resulting from modern man's inability to deal openly and personally with the fact of death."[28] I am presuming that people have had their share of trust, love, intimacy and generativity and so are ready for hope. When men have experienced both sides of life then *words* of hope can buttress the instinct of hope against despair. An adult knows that dependence and independence, joy and sorrow, hope and despair are inseparable parts of experience. At that point of time one can begin *talking* about death and resurrection; before then it can only be lived and not talked about because talking would rip apart what is one. "Many endeavored

27. Allport, *The Individual and His Religion,* p. 37.
28. Thomas Ogletree, "From Anxiety to Responsibility: The Shifting Focus of Theological Reflection," in *New Theology* # 6, ed. Martin Marty and Dean Peerman (New York, 1969), p. 49.

in vain joyfully to speak profoundest joy; here at last in the tragic, I see it expressed" (Hölderlin).

The topic of death should not be exaggerated here lest it again be ripped from its context. However, death does function as central to religious faith and the treatment of death is symptomatic of the overall attitude of religion. A childish or adolescent attitude toward death will probably be connected with a generally inhuman and dehumanizing religion.

Christianity has led the way in emphasizing the individual person and the particular events of history. These were great contributions of Christianity that should not be put aside today. There is perhaps some danger of this occurring. But this stress upon the particular must come up from below, by an all inclusive rather than an all exclusive kind of uniqueness and by an understanding of the individual not as an isolate but as the matrix of relationships. A Western Christian has a great deal to learn from other faiths about the unity of himself with the universe. At the same time, he could give an example of the fact that a strong sense of the uniqueness of person is compatible with a receptive, communal and reverent attitude toward the world. An adult faith should reject collectivism and individualism as part of the same alternative. The other alternative is a faith in which the individual saves his life by losing it. When a man can discover his brotherhood with other men, the animals, the trees and the rivers, then he can be a full individual whose uniqueness is in no way threatened by his union with all things.

Perhaps no one has so pointedly elaborated a conception of Christian faith as Søren Kierkegaard. With great stress upon becoming an individual, Kierkegaard saw faith as the living before God with the unresolved tension of necessity and freedom, finitude and infinity. His notion of faith is rightly criticized for its lack of social framework, although given the times he lived in the deficiency may be understandable. Kierkegaard's central insight remains true: the need for a faith which knows itself as struggling toward the unity of contrasting opposites.

"Faith is: that the self in being itself and in willing to be itself is grounded transparently in God . . . And for the whole of Christianity it is one of the most decisive definitions that the opposite of sin is not virtue but faith."[29]

A Christian theology must never lose touch with this central experience of faith. A theology for adults would be one that tentatively experiments in formulations of human experience in quest of the infinite. The experience is certain but the formulations are the fallible expressions of the human mind. A theology works out of a tradition and must try to maintain contact with these roots in the past. But human continuity, as opposed to logical continuity, has more flexibility and gaps than theology has ever allowed itself. Theology should always be tentative and the church, as a whole, ought to give it room for wrong turns. "A modern theologian," writes Edward Schillebeeckx, "may feel secure as a believer and yet *hesitant* as a theologian—in this he is respecting the mystery. One is sometimes bound to wonder whether the certainty of some theologians does not conceal a hesitant *faith*."[30] I shall come back in the last chapter to the connection between an experienced faith (fidelity) and the elaboration of a faith expression (theology).

To understand the difference between experience of faith and knowledge of dogma, to accept doubt as part of faith, to understand tolerance as intrinsic to a faith conviction, Christian theology should be studied in conjunction with other religious traditions. For those who fear that such a study will lead to a "loss of faith" among Christians it can be said that this is a minor danger. Certainly, apathy, ignorance and prejudice are much greater dangers. The study of another's faith often does lead to a conversion but the conversion is not to the other's position. It

29. Søren Kierkegaard, *Fear and Trembling & The Sickness Unto Death* (Garden City, 1954), p. 213.
30. Edward Schillebeeckx, *God the Future of Man* (New York, 1968), p. 19.

is a conversion to the truth which goes beyond all individual faiths and is embodied in each life.[31]

The study of religion is an integral part of any well-rounded education. As I have indicated in the previous chapter, such a study may begin in early elementary school, emerging as part of the study of history, literature and social science. A course on religion itself does not seem feasible before the later years of high school. It is possible in many circumstances to teach a respectable course on the subject before students leave high school and this is in fact going on in some schools.[32] More properly, however, the actual course on the comparison of religions belongs in the university. Religion as the culmination of study need not be the very last thing to be begun after every other study is complete. But it should have ample preparation through the study of disciplines that are normally carried out in the university. Some acquaintance with philosophy, psychology, sociology and anthropology is a decided help in understanding the place of religious faith in the life of man.[33]

The study of religion does not produce committed believers in any religious tradition. At every level study has to be complemented by a living context and a practice of belief. So long as religion functions in an academic setting it has to retain the "objective" character spoken of previously. In the short run this kind of treatment is not good for getting proselytes or increasing devotions. In the long run, however, it can initiate a process of continued interest in religious faith as an ever widening and deepening search for the ultimate truth of our lives.

31. See the remarks of Dr. Faruqui in *The Word in the Third World,* ed. James Cotter (Washington, 1968), p. 169.
32. See Joseph Forcinelli, "The Study of World Religions in the American High School," in *Religious Education,* 64 (Mar. Apr., 1969), pp. 108–112.
33. See Ernest Becker, *Beyond Alienation* (New York, 1967).

7. Conclusions for Catholicism

THROUGHOUT the preceding pages I have made a number of suggestions for change in the Catholic church's approach to religious education. In this last chapter I would like to pull together these recommendations into a coordinated program of change addressed to all segments of the church population. Unless there is coordinated effort, changes in one part of a system may only aggravate difficulties in the rest of the system. One cannot advocate professional salaries for members of religious orders and at the same time pretend that Catholic schools can do business as usual. One cannot advocate closing Catholic schools and having all religion taught in the home unless one has a way to deal with parents who feel inadequate to such a task. The church is like an ecological system in which the problem is not one element or another, but the balanced distribution and harmonious interaction of the elements.

These conclusions are addressed specifically to the Roman Catholic church. I have seldom differentiated in this book between Protestant and Catholic. Indeed, the book advocates moving toward a point at which all discussions and decisions of Christians would be made not only in cooperation with one another but in cooperation with non-Christians as well. Realistically, however, cooperation in educational institutions is at a beginning stage and it takes much longer to transform institutions than to change ideas. Catholic and Protestant institutions ought to get together and a few of them are doing that. The fact remains that the Roman Catholic church is still a highly distinctive element in religious education and a very visible part of general education in America. To single out people in the

Catholic church who have an interest in education does not take us from the ecumenical path if our aim is to awaken ecumenical attitudes in these people and to encourage ecumenical decisions in the church.

The American Catholic church's investment in education is one of the wonders of the modern world. The multi-billion dollar enterprise is unparalleled by other religious bodies or by the Catholic church elsewhere in history. Anyone recommending drastic change in these institutions should first acknowledge the strength and greatness of this tradition. Many reformers of religious education grow impatient at the slowness of change in the massive educational systems of the church, particularly on the East coast and in other large cities. Impatience may be in order but if so it should be clearly differentiated from an anti-institutionalism that is much better at destroying than at building. As long as the church has people, buildings, money, interest, tradition, etc., something positive (and necessarily "institutional") ought to be attempted with these resources. Attacking the school system has no long term future, whether or not the attack is successful; nor is closing schools a positive educational policy. However, the use of excessive energy, pressure and persuasion to get outside aid for an under-financed school system can also be myopic.

The suggestions in this chapter do not pretend to deal with all of the complex issues surrounding the Catholic school system today. Consideration here is restricted to religious education which is only one factor in the school system. However, since many people seem to assume that the teaching of religion is the very *raison d'être* of the Catholic schools the issue should be carefully examined. Otherwise, it is not unheard of for people to work harder and harder at an end which is no longer worth attaining.

The religious education question in the American Catholic church is related to every aspect of church life. Changing religious education in the church is equivalent to changing the

145

church. There is no point in berating school superintendents or attacking religion teachers as if they either had produced the problems or could now remedy the situation. No one group can supply the needed change although some steps can be taken by each group. Ultimately, the problem comes down to whether the church is an institution which is sufficiently credible to inspire trust and confidence.

The church is not alone, of course, in the challenge being made to the institutions of society. This challenge is particularly severe, however, for any institution which makes exalted claims for itself. The church points to qualities which it calls superhuman but many other people see simply as inhuman. Every institution has some degree of what Keniston calls the "institutionalization of hypocrisy."[1] This element is both a necessity for survival and a driving force for change. This fact of life in the church is difficult for the old guard to admit and painful for reformers to live with. But admitting and accepting the gap between the ideal and the institutionalization of it is necessary for both survival and change.

When we talk about changing the institutions of the church or the institution of the church itself, we are talking about ourselves. There is not a collection of offices, financial reports, and buildings which constitute an "institutional church" as opposed to a personal church. There are not a few men in high places who constitute a "them" to be attacked by us. A systemic problem requires systematic change. Any criticism of office holders or attack upon specific decisions must be for the sake of creating better institutional patterns to serve life. Attacks cannot be launched on the premise that it is possible to have a world in which there are no mistakes, restrictions and failures.

Education has been understood in this book as the improvement of human life through the devising of structures for learning. Almost anything can function as an educational instrument if it serves this aim of human development. In this regard, the

1. See Kenneth Keniston, *Young Radicals* (New York, 1968), p. 237.

church as a whole ought to be an educational force for humanity, that is, one of the environments or structures of learning for mankind. At the same time, the church in its entirety should be the context for the Christian people's growth in religious understanding. As the church looks to the former and larger of these tasks, it might find itself doing the latter job better. Concentration of educational energies aimed at church membership would almost certainly be self-defeating. The church's educational mission does not consist in running schools (though some schools may at some times be helpful to that end) but in being a church that educates by being itself.

The church has many factors in its favor as it looks both at education and its own nature, but the elements need realignment and release. If the church actually functioned as a community of people dedicated to searching for the divine, reflecting on the implications of the quest, and living by the consequences of the reflection, its whole mode of operation would be educational. The Roman Catholic church does not succeed very well on this account because it lacks com-union, the sharing of educative experience by equals. Education, of course, does include some inequalities; for example, it is usually presumed that a professor has more knowledge or at least greater training in the use of resources than does the student. Underlying all inequalities, however, there must be a more fundamental equality of all men before the bar of human experience. Such equality includes the recognition that any man may see a truth which is worth sharing with all men. Whenever this principle of equality is violated there will be protest in one form or another ranging from a sullen look on a child's face to the burning down of a university. The protest is often in the name of "freedom" but, as many commentators have noted, it is more accurately seen as a demand for self-dignity and the integrity of experience.

Schools are in constant danger of violating this equality and integrity. Professors can easily begin to think of themselves as possessors of knowledge to be dispensed rather than as humble

147

interpreters of experience. Fortunately for everyone, professors must sometimes take off their professorial gowns and go home to the family or mix with other people on a simpler human basis. In addition, their role as teacher is one that is acquired through some skill and one that is exercised in interaction with a community. The more competent they are in the role of teacher, the more they will realize that they are part of a community struggling toward a truth which no one possesses but all can share.

In many ways the Catholic church finds itself in direct contradiction to these elements of community, education and teaching. There has been failure to develop adequate institutional means to carry out the work of the church. This fact is most striking in the rhetoric which surrounds the "teaching office" of the bishop. It is amazing how this issue is still gingerly sidestepped in Catholic writing. The assumption that there is a collection of truths revealed by God that are dispensed by the church is slowly disappearing. The corollary to that belief, namely, that within the church the bishops are the dispensers of such truths, goes on unchecked. The power that is attributed to the church "magisterium" is, to say the least, problematic. In any case, it bears little connection to what is today called teaching. Making the bishops the church's teachers on the basis of Christ's commands to the apostles is little short of equivocation. John McKenzie notes that "when the New Testament uses the word *didaskein* (teach) and its cognates, it is safe to say that the words never mean the kind of 'authoritative teaching' which is treated in modern theology."[2]

There is no personal attack here upon bishops nor attack upon the office of episcopacy. As the world more and more "implodes" on itself the roles of episcopacy and papacy will probably increase in significance. There is real value in having bishops as points of unity in a community or as spokesmen of the gospel for a national church. The need for leadership has by no means

2. John L. McKenzie, *Authority in the Church* (New York, 1966), p. 78.

decreased although every institution is having its troubles today in discovering how leaders should lead. For example, labor unions have always had this problem. Practically by definition, a labor union official is no longer a laborer. How does one speak *for* people when one is no longer *of* them? No one can detail all the things that a leader should do in order to lead. It has become clear, however, that there are some things he must not do. The most obvious thing that a leader must not do is to claim to have a special source of knowledge that can be used unilaterally to end questions. He would also be advised not to assume titles, dress and living style which establish differences from the community on the basis of external insignia rather than by competence, dedication and courage in carrying a common burden.

The episcopal role is to devise ways to preserve the gospel of Jesus Christ. The living of that gospel, the teaching of religion, and the spread of the church are not the tasks of the bishop but the work of Christian churches. If the bishop is trying to be a gathering point and mediator of all forces of the church, he may be doing all that is possible. One can also demand that a bishop preserve the gospel by exemplifying it in his life but at that point we return to what is shared in common with all Christians.

The supposition that the bishop is the teacher of the diocese and that religion teachers in the schools are an extension of the bishop is simply a fallacy that must be put to rest. This would be true even were the work of these teachers a catechizing of Christian faith. But the case is rendered obvious by the fact that these teachers are actually teaching an ecumenical course of study. Teachers of religion ought to be judged for their competence on the same basis as any other teachers. Ordinarily, a bishop would have no more talent for making such judgments than anyone else outside the school. Some teachers deserve to be fired, some courses in religion ought to be dropped; but having educational policy directed by agents of a chancery is a ridiculously inappropriate procedure. In recent years, teachers in

Catholic colleges have been reaching the point of having "academic freedom" in the teaching of religion. The Catholic hierarchy, reluctantly in many cases, has had to acknowledge the right of the university to set its own policy and judge its own faculty. This freedom from outside pressures does not yet exist on primary and secondary levels of education. Episcopal committees still claim the right to examine religion textbooks and force out teachers who are not properly docile.

It should be clear that I am not saying that all the new catechetical books are of excellent quality (I think most of them are dreadful) or that all religion teachers are doing their jobs perfectly. I am simply saying that the Catholic hierarchy has no particular competence in judging these matters. The words orthodoxy and heresy are still meaningful terms which refer to the ability of the church community to survive with the integrity of belief. This is a question for the whole adult community to struggle with but it is a question which does not arise until there is a developed exposition of Christian doctrine. As soon as one gives up trying to indoctrinate children with truths of faith, then the issue of orthodoxy ceases to be relevant for them. In the framework which I have presented here, and which to varying degrees is operative already, Christianity is not the subject of teaching. This fact is what the textbook critics ought to charge instead of finding in the books all varieties of heresy.

The misuse of episcopal power is really not the problem but a symptom of the much deeper problem of church structure. A community needs structure, an organization needs leadership, a society needs authority. But the church, like so many other groups today, suffers from a lack of imagination in getting people together, establishing communication and making decisions. The establishing of committees is at best only a small part of a solution; used in isolation, the proliferation of committees and councils will probably add to autocracy rather than diminish it. Whether or not one man is finally the decision maker is not so important as *how* he makes the decision. The process most to watch is the means by which leadership is attained. If the leader of a body does not come up from a body through the exercise of the body's powers, then that body is in trouble. The leader can talk all he wishes about "delegating" power (a term which presumes he has it to bestow) or collegial responsibility but it will be a charade. The question of a national pastoral council being advisory or deliberative on church matters is mostly academic. The important question is the amount and kind of power this body has over who comes to be a bishop in the future.

More than appointment of councils from on high, the reform of religious education requires growth of communities from below. It remains to be seen whether this upward growth can take place without a toppling of the existing structure. I think it would be tragic if Catholics were to lose contact with the rich heritage of their past. There is an acute danger of this loss occurring unless those who are trying to build something new and those who are trying to preserve something old can tolerate some differences and keep open some communication. In referring to Christian communities springing up from below I do not mean "underground churches" but the quite visible and open gathering of any groups that are trying to pray, play, work and learn together.

Such communities are indispensable to learning, especially in the religious area, because they provide release from the emotional block to systematic inquiry. The immediate, personal and affective dimension of faith is what I call fidelity. The church community itself should be religiously educational by providing an experience of fidelity. The word faith is not beyond salvage but the word fidelity catches the tenor of what happens in interaction with others. Faith need not but often does designate an impersonal thing, that is, a content of abstractions. Fidelity, in contrast, connotes a personal relation that includes a tug at our feelings. "Fidelity," Erikson writes, "is the ability to sustain loyalties freely pledged in spite of the inevitable contradictions of value systems."[3] One could speak about teaching the faith but it is difficult to imagine someone saying that he was teaching fidelity. Nevertheless, fidelity is central to the educational enterprise and may turn out to be the element that keeps human life going at all. In a society in which all systems are tending to become temporary, partial and mobile, fidelity to other persons becomes almost the sole constant in life.[4] This fidelity arises from the experience of concrete, individual people. What we need is an experiencing of the human as human, an encountering of the rich, puzzling, promising, frustrating, frightening diversity of mankind. In the meeting with a few persons there can be discovered the meaning of the human race as one and yet diverse, and the reality of myself as one and yet diverse. When humanness is penetrated in depth then there is a discovery that reality may be painful but is bearable, that freedom is good though frightening and that social change is necessary though ambiguous.

Whenever people meet on a plane of fidelity to each other, a process is set in motion (what Kurt Lewin called "unfreezing") that makes all kinds of dramatic change possible. This reference is not exclusively or primarily to sensitivity training but to any community where people are willing to put their persons on the line in an educational experience. The key condition is the absence of threat to the self structure. Then, experience can be perceived in differentiated fashion and the structure of the self can be revised to assimilate such experience. This move is not a psychologizing of religious education nor a dabbling in current fads. The laboratory experience uses techniques similar to those which the church has used over the centuries in parish life or religious orders but which the church has failed to develop in accord with the times.

Without an experience of fidelity it is doubtful that any

3. Erikson, *Insight and Responsibility*, p. 125.
4. See Warren Bennis and P. E. Slater, *The Temporary Society* (New York, 1968), p. 128.

educational program is going to change people much. People may say that they are searching for faith but it will only be a search for one answer rather than another. No one can let go and start searching unless there is someone there to catch him, not someone who knows the answers but someone who cares for him. Henri Nouwen writes: "Trust creates the possibility of a religion of search which makes a commitment possible without certainty."[5] This last phrase is interesting, even if ambiguous. It is pointing out that in one sense there is no certainty in faith and that this is what one must come to accept about faith. But to do just that, there must be an experience of fidelity which is certain, an experience that some other person (and by implication every person) is real, good and trustworthy. In this terminology the certainty of fidelity and the certainty of faith can vary in almost inverse proportion. To reach a state of being sure of who one is in relation to others is to reach a state of being able to doubt any proposition one holds. A person can search the world for faith only when he can rely upon a fidelity that has come home.

The centrality of fidelity does not necessarily mean that religion courses must be preceded by T-group sessions. It does mean, at the least, that far more attention must be paid to how people come together in formal education and in church groups. Apparently minor things can make a big difference in learning; for example, knowing the name of the person next to you, having a quiet and relaxing room arrangement, mixing freely with teachers outside of the academic atmosphere. So much effort is wasted in trying to teach religion to people who are not in a position where they can unfreeze. They cannot hear answers which anyone is offering because they are psychologically incapable of asking the questions in a personal way.

In addition to the experience of fidelity and usually concomitant with it, is the other aspect of religious education,

5. Henri Nouwen, *Intimacy: Pastoral Psychological Studies* (Notre Dame, 1969), p. 17.

namely, the vision of faith. In psychological terms, unfreezing has as its counterpart the process of scanning and imitation. Once a fluidity is introduced and alteration is possible there is a positive impulse toward looking to the horizon for new possibilities and noticing the behavior of other individuals worth imitating. In biblical terms, repentance and conversion lead to faith and discipleship. The relationship is not entirely unilateral. The experience of fidelity precedes the elaboration of a faith but the vision of faith in turn makes possible a deeper experience of others. John Gardner has remarked that the creative individual can probably only tolerate a wild disorder of ideas and experiences because he is confident that at some point he can impose on them some pattern of symbols.[6] Ideas, words, and conceptual patterns, even if not certain, can create a framework within which more and more experience can emerge. What is symbolized can sooner or later be realized either in art or in life.

For this reason, Christian teachers must continue to elaborate a theology. The fact that it is for smaller numbers of people would not diminish its significance. Theology must continually draw upon common experience but it must, without apology, use disciplined tools of the mind to push beyond that beginning. Today, there are many people who see no value to speculation. "The obscurantists of all ages," writes A. N. Whitehead, "exhibit the same principles. All common sense is within them. The only serious antagonist is History and the history of Europe is dead against them. Abstract speculation has been the salvation of the world—speculation which made systems and then transcended them, speculations which ventured to the furthest limit of abstraction."[7]

The elaboration of this speculative inquiry is a disciplined work of the mind. I am not in favor of forcing people into school for long periods, but when they are there of their own free wills, something definite, prepared and disciplined ought to happen.

6. John Gardner, *No Easy Victories* (New York, 1968), p. 121.
7. A. N. Whitehead, *The Function of Reason* (Boston, 1958), pp. 75 ff.

There is a danger that schools are frittering away their necessary form in rear guard action. Lectures become meandering monologues, seminars become interminable bull sessions and programs of study are programmed in name only. The problem is especially acute in the area of religion. The Catholic institution is caught between its conscientious conviction that it must do something for the religious life of its students, and the painful but patent fact that most of the students will positively resist a course on religion. Very often, the result is a compromise but one which satisfies no one and fools no one.

The school in its own kind way is trying to lessen the pain by diluting the time, the form and the subject matter. However, the move is clearly a holding action which has no future and does not succeed well even in the present. The students are at first grateful for the change but their relief quickly gives way to resentment that they are being forced to put up with something which even the faculty and administration do not believe in. The students are surely correct in protesting the school's two-faced ness, that is, its endless rhetoric which everyone knows is at variance with reality. If someone believes in something he speaks of it passionately and not half heartedly; he teaches it demandingly and not lackadaisically. A passion for the truth is not incompatible with an open, ecumenical attitude; rather, passionate involvement is inherent to an ecumenical search for faith. There is a false irenicism in the air which equates tolerance and nondiscrimination of ideas. All opinions being accepted as true means that no opinion is worth holding as significant. Referring to the benevolent polytheism of the Roman Empire, Edward Gibbon wrote: "All religions were to the people equally true, to the philosophers equally false, and to the government equally useful."

The remedy for our predicament surely lies in the direction of offering a worthwhile course of studies for those people who want it. As I have pointed out earlier, the interest in religion may not come until a person is 40 or 50 years old. If this be true, then all the gimmicks in the world are not going to make it work for high school sophomores. People of all ages need help which in some sense is religious, but they ought to have a course on religion only when there is sufficient preparation and interest for it. If religion is to be offered in the Catholic high school, perhaps it should be an honors course in senior year. A person would feel it to be an accomplishment to qualify for the course. Only by a dramatic move of this kind can the element of coercion be removed which still hangs over religion courses in Catholic schools.

In any case, we need an experience of fidelity in church community and educational institution. To strengthen that experience we need a vision of faith that stretches the mind outward. The need for such meaning will not decrease as life goes on. As long as it can return to the simple base of experienced love and fidelity, the search for faith and the will to meaning will continue to grow throughout adult life. Those who survive the difficult world of the future will be those who continue to learn throughout life. Forcing children and adolescents to learn their religion so that they will have their faith runs counter to what is needed.

As I have indicated in Chapter 4, parents hold a crucial position in religious education. It is they who are most influential in providing early experiences of fidelity that can eventually lead to faith. The work of church leaders should not be directed toward the parent giving religious instruction but to the parent being a parent. There are some skills of communication which parents need. Possibly we should have courses in preparation for a "parent career."[8] A mother need not think of herself as a catechist with an additional mission of teaching religion to the child. As a matter of fact, much of the effort with parents today has to be directed to convincing them not to teach religion to their children. The amount of religion that adults try to teach children will vary in almost inverse proportion to how much the

8. See Fantini and Weinstein, *op. cit.*, p. 41.

adults themselves understand their religion. Very little help is being offered to adults to come to this mature understanding of their own faith. Theology courses for parents would have the effect of cutting down the Christian doctrine lessons for children and increasing the "primitive religious education" that children need.

People interested in religious education should try changing some of the environmental conditions under which children grow up. The child of the ghetto suffers one kind of deprivation which is fairly easy to locate. The suburban child, isolated with the over-attentive mother, is exposed to other cultural disadvantages. We do not need special religious education for either suburban or urban children but we do need other alternatives in the community situation available to people. In particular, children need more adults about them than the two parents. The isolation of the nuclear family is a problem often commented upon but still not widely understood.[9] The church might provide some small help to deal with the problem and in some instances it may be succeeding already This concern should be brought to the center of discussion on religious education for children. To whatever degree possible the church might cooperate with other religious groups and public agencies to establish day care centers for children. Tens of thousands of small children badly need "religious education", that is, the presence of adults who care for them and provide for them a healthy learning situation.

Religious orders have played a key role in religious education, and, despite their shaky condition today, they continue to be an important element in this picture. The religious orders still have the resources to do some new and imaginative things to cope with the religious education problem. Unfortunately, they seem to be disintegrating just at the time that the church and the country could benefit from communities of people in dedicated work. The multiple problems that afflict them cannot be discussed in

9. See Slater, *op. cit.*, pp. 141–143.

detail here.[10] However, one part of the problem is that many people have come into religious orders to work at religious education. They are put into classrooms to teach religion to children who are unprepared to learn. Their other alternative is to work at CCD which is usually badly financed, understaffed and unorganized. Either alternative is enough to make a man look for work at AT & T or IBM.

The religious orders, I have urged, ought to disengage themselves *qua* orders from the Catholic school system. Members of orders who wish to continue teaching in the remaining Catholic schools should be free to do so. The salaries of religious ought to be the same as lay teachers and the order could then decide to subsidize those schools which the members wish to help. Other members of religious orders could work in public education, social work, government, or anything they choose. In time this would allow some members of religious orders to work in religious education. They could do needed work with parents and small children, in universities, with old people, or in public schools.

In addition, the religious order should be able to sponsor flexible centers of religious learning either in connection with universities or as autonomous institutions. By their getting rid of buildings no longer serving a useful purpose and by their members receiving full salaries, religious orders would have the financial resources to run a few of their own operations. Whatever be the problems of religious orders, a lack of money should not be their big difficulty. Yet, as a matter of fact, lack of money to educate people for their work, to support them in new ventures, to retrain them for second careers, and to retire them with some security, is a large part of what is killing religious orders. Books on religious life continue to talk about what poverty really means. Religious superiors continue to accept what they think is the minimum they need to survive. It is like a man starving to death who consoles himself in his pains with the

10. See my *The New Community* (New York, 1970).

thought that he is saving food. If religious orders were to begin deciding for themselves what to do, enormous changes could take place in religious education.

Catholic schools which continue to exist must work in continually closer cooperation with public education. They must realize that their *raison d'être* will not be found in the teaching of religion but in the running of an institution that serves the human and religious needs of the whole community. As has often been commented upon, a Catholic (or any other nonpublic) school which serves any need not currently met by public education has a purpose for being.[11] Some zealous supporters of Catholic schools imply that they exist to teach religion and that if religion courses were taken out of these schools they would be useless. I think that many of these schools are much better than their supporters give them credit for and that they would be and are worthwhile schools apart from religion courses taught in them. Competition can be a healthy factor in education. However, where Catholic schools are serving a need that should be met by the larger community, they can fulfill this function only by being a prod to the public conscience and by being willing to self-destruct when there is a better way to meet a social need.

Religious education ought to be clearly distinguished from the question of Catholic schools. Whether a Catholic school ought to continue or not involves many factors, only one of which is religious education. A conclusive argument for the Catholic school cannot be made on the basis that it is the place where religious education happens. No one can deny that existing religious education programs outside the Catholic school are shaky enterprises. The past is clear enough but it does not specify our future. After the federal government spends tens of billions of dollars on highways and a trickle of money on mass transit, no one should be surprised that there are good highways to drive on

11. See Albert Koob and Russell Shaw, *S.O.S. For Catholic Schools* (New York, 1970), pp. 103–126.

and almost no railroads. This fact, however, does nothing to prove that mass transit will not work. It does not even prove that the federal highway program has not been a colossal disaster.

Too many arguments have been fought over whether CCD programs, if given a few more bandaids, could duplicate the work of Catholic schools. Those who have sided with the CCD in such disputes have been in the hopeless position of trying to maintain against all evidence that an hour per week of poorly managed instruction could accomplish what a school does. They were wrong, of course, in what they were arguing for but they were right in their instinctive claim that there is something wrong with a church that is today sinking nearly all its resources into a school system. I repeat that I am not against Catholic schools but for the sake of the Catholic school's self-understanding and self-justification it must relate itself to the needs of the total community. It cannot claim the right to exist because it teaches religion better than existing CCD programs.

The objection to questioning the existence of Catholic schools remains: where would one teach religion? My answer is supplied by this book. I would hope at the least to have broadened the nature of the discussion so that one need not propose an alternate quasi-Catholic school system. Some people's minds get fixed in one groove which prevents them from seeing the *kind* of proposal that is at issue. One could still argue against the proposal as false or incorrect but not on the basis that the proposal is "impractical." What I mean is illustrated by the following exchange of dialogue that I have been involved in dozens of times. Question: How do you teach the sacrament of penance to a third grader? Answer: You don't. It is impossible. Stop teaching it. Question: I agree with you in theory but what do you teach in practice? Answer: Nothing. Question: I understand all that theory but my problem is *how* do you teach it? Answer: There's no answer to that question. Question: That's the trouble with you theorizers. You don't know the practical difficulties of teaching the third grade. When is someone going to do something practical and come out with good lesson plans for teaching penance to third graders?

The conversation recorded above does not go anywhere because there is a difference of models and premises. The fruitlessness of the exchange does not come from one party being theoretical and the other being practical minded. Not teaching penance is a practical suggestion for which no teacher's handbook is necessary. There are, admittedly, practical problems connected with this policy but they are not practical problems of religious education. It may be a practical problem for myself if I lose my job of being a religion teacher. It may be a practical problem for myself if a religious superior can order me to teach third grade religion. Such problems ought to be kept distinct from questions of how to teach religion.

Whether CCD is a category that is salvageable is highly doubtful. Newly developing programs may be hindered by being placed under the CCD heading. The attempt to run schools under conditions in which schools are impossible has given a bad name to CCD. The danger now is that having failed at grammar school, high school and college level, dioceses are taking on the adult world with similar tools and the same mentality. The church, as I pointed out in Chapter 6, is in a slightly better position in approaching adults simply because competing structures for adults are so underdeveloped. Thus, there is an advantage in moving into this near virgin territory but also, by the same token, there is a need for massive infusions of people, money, ideas and hard work. Current indications are that very few dioceses are ready to make such an investment. While business goes on as usual at the expensive Catholic school and the unworkable CCD school, a flood of rhetoric develops about the church's concern with the infant in the ghetto, the young parent in suburbia, the student in the secular university, welfare mothers, old people, etc. The resources, however, are ridiculously disproportionate to the pretenses of programs.

The inadequacy is apparent in most of the jobs set up under the title "parish coordinator." Sometimes the job carries a good salary but the coordinator finds that he has nothing to coordinate: no people, no money, no programs, no support. The coordinator of the religion program often finds that he *is* the religion program. I repeatedly warn graduate students that if a pastor is hiring them to be parish coordinator, it is probably either for the best or the worst of reasons and they had better find out beforehand which it is. Some pastors are in the business of looking for a scapegoat ("Let's see what magic this fellow can work—or else"). Other pastors know they are in trouble and are genuinely looking for someone to do whatever can be done. Even with these best of parish situations, however, one must wonder if the job is workable. The job may be impossible because the present parish structure is impossible. That question cannot be pursued here but some immediate steps must be taken lest the intelligent, educated and dedicated people all disappear from the scene.

The Catholic church should not be putting people into parish coordinator jobs unless there is a willingness to get educated people, to support them by shifting church resources, and to consider changing the parochial structure as a new pattern of education evolves. The present deficient attitude is exemplified by a diocese wishing to begin a program of religion coordinators and asking each religious order to assign someone to the work. The diocese's interest in this area extends only as far as buying nuns' services because they are cheap. In addition to being an insult to sisters, the policy is not designed to improve religious education. People need extensive and expensive preparation in schools of theology and education. They then need support on a regional basis to avoid their being isolated and to provide them with resources to do their work. Eventually, for a director of education's job to be meaningful, he must share the directing job of the community or parish. Instead of a pastor and his flock we shall have a community with a small team of leaders (men and women) to direct liturgy, education, social action, etc. Until the Catholic community is ready to start moving in that direction, it is doubtful that they should simply repeat the Protestant pattern of getting a young woman to be Director of Religious Education in each parish. This system, with the D.R.E. having no real power except to take care of the children, can hardly be called a notable success.

Religious education concerns what goes on in families and on the streets, rent laws, zoning ordinances, police regulations, health requirements, city planning, etc. The concern with these things is "religious education" in a legitimate sense of that term. Religious education is also concerned, of course, with what goes on in schools. Catholic schools are places of religious education but in ways hardly suspected by the school administration. The school policy on dress for girls and haircuts for boys can sometimes be more influential and certainly is more symptomatic than what is taught in religion classes. Schools of their nature seem gravely exposed to the "institutionalization of hypocrisy." This is not a reason for closing schools nor for berating all schools in general and Catholic schools in particular. It is an invitation for people interested in religious education to look at the whole school's attitude toward the almost defenseless student.

One good thing about religion classes, I have pointed out, is that they may present an opportunity for raising questions about the school which the school does not allow anywhere else. This is the "compensatory role" which religion courses at any level can play in present education. For example, the kind of open forum which William Glasser suggests for schools is quite possible in the religion class of Catholic schools.[12] In fact, many religion teachers have been using such a procedure for some time. At times the contribution can be in the form of new subject matter

12. William Glasser, *Schools Without Failures* (New York, 1969), pp. 122–185.

163

which does not fit existing curriculums. For example, film study made early inroads into Catholic schools via the religion class. Likewise, while it will probably take years to make ecology the core of educational curriculums, many ecological discussions have already entered Catholic schools in religion classes.

In calling this a compensatory function I am admitting that this is not the ideal way to get open discussions, film, ecology, or anything else into a school. Too much faddishness and too little concern for the integrity of the thing itself are likely to accompany such *ad hoc* uses of a religion course. Nevertheless, this kind of thing is happening and under the direction of careful teachers it can be a contribution to education. Teachers of religion in Catholic schools might take a little hope if they could see this contribution they are making. If they cannot be content with this role, then perhaps they should look for a situation in which they can teach a serious course of religion to people who want to study it. I have suggested that such a course might be given as early as upper high school but that it belongs more properly to university and post-university study.

Religious education is also at issue in everything that happens in the public school. Eventually it will be possible to teach religion within history, social science or literature. People connected with Catholic schools or churches should be looking forward to cooperation in this venture. For the present, and continuing in the future, religious education concerns the overall style, atmosphere and operation of the public school. A theology that respects the integrity of the secular is not interested in seeing religious trappings in the school. It is interested in seeing human beings respected, loved and educated. George Albert Coe many years ago wrote: "Give us public schools that develop active interest in human welfare, passion for the basal rights of man, faith in the capacity of men for unselfishness, and the heart and purpose of cooperation—give us public schools like these, and social religion will look upon them as doing God's will even though they do not name his name, but only that of his children."[13] What we need so badly is schools that are truly "public." Just as "catholic" school is often a misnomer, so also many schools are not public in the sense of being open to all people and all concerns. Schools are often segregated ghettos of racial, religious, economic, or social groups. One of the reasons for working toward the introduction of religion into a school would be to make it a truly public school, that is, an institution capable of dealing with the full spectrum of human concerns.[14]

The Catholic college over the years has moved toward making religion or theology an elective. Not many colleges have gone all the way in establishing religion on its own as an intellectually respectable field to be taught to people who are interested in it. Most colleges have reduced requirements and added elective courses but a framework of required credits continues. It is not clear that the cutting back of requirements has come from a conviction to decrease quantity while increasing quality or from a battle of attrition in face of rising student complaints.

Catholic colleges went through a period in the 1950's of changing from religion departments to theology departments. Now they are changing their theology departments to religion. This move is not a turning back of the clock; many of the people who fought against religion departments in the past are the people fighting for them today. In part this reflects the changing meaning of the word religion in college circles though it also reflects the ambiguity in the word religion itself. The religion that was formerly taught by Catholic colleges was largely the primitive variety of adherence to practices and beliefs inculcated in childhood. The religion that is re-emerging in the college today is the ecumenical and critical study of the phenomenon of religion. It would be unfortunate if colleges gave up the study of Christian theology, although in Catholic colleges there is little likelihood of that

13. George Albert Coe, *A Social Theory of Religious Education* (New York, 1917), p. 264.
14. See Harvey Cox, "The Relation between Religion and Education," in *Region and Public Education,* ed. Theodore Sizer (Boston, 1967), pp. 99–111.

occurring. Christian theology should be one of the offerings within a program of religious studies. Such a department should be able to exist in both church related colleges and public universities. The danger in Catholic colleges today is that too few people have thought out a position on the relation of religion and theology. The religion faculty is not clear on its own role. The professors' confusion, of course, is raised exponentially at the level of college administrators, alumni and chancery officials.

Even more than student complaints, the cause of the reduction of religion requirements is the need to "secularize" the college's appearance for state and federal aid. The maneuver may not be a bad one; it may not even be dishonest. It does raise the question of whether many such colleges should exist. The question of whether they *can* exist is implicit in the appeal for public aid. Whether or not the move is successful remains to be seen. It does seem probable that many church related colleges will eventually pass over into a state system. Before doing so or in the process of doing so, several colleges might consider creating an ecumenical center of religion/theology. Such a center could cooperate with the university in serving the whole community. The last act of the Catholic college could be among the best acts of its life.

One has to be a little pessimistic about this change occurring. Getting several colleges to cooperate on such a venture involves great amounts of red tape. Ecumenical complexes have been launched in San Francisco, Chicago and Boston. Perhaps this kind of thing is a more realistic hope than expecting Catholic colleges and seminaries to initiate cooperation (the Catholic women's colleges in Chicago would be a notable exception). Despite the rhetoric about interest in matters theological and religious, Catholic colleges have been notoriously indifferent to the quality of education in religion within themselves. Certainly, they have shown little tendency to invest any money in that area.

The Catholic church in America, despite its increasing financial difficulties, still has great resources in its institutions and its people. This is hardly a time for discouragement though it is a time for making a few dramatic shifts to prevent the growth of frustration among people engaged in religious education. The basic change must come in the area of ecclesiastical structure through a move toward democratization of the church. The full realization of this step will be a long and painful process. The religious education changes will be mostly a consequence of the change in church structure but education will rebound in effect upon its own antecedent cause.

As many parochial schools close, it is to be hoped that Catholic communities will not lose the strong commitment they have had to education. The energy has to be redirected to new forms, both to existing public education and to new forms of education for old and young. Many Catholic schools and/or churches could be turned into community centers of education. The Catholic church in America has sometimes been ridiculed for building a school before a church in many parishes. The instinct was not entirely misplaced. Catholics arriving in America realized that the church could not survive in this new world without a well educated membership. The principle is more true today than ever but the situation of education has changed in the past century. In order to be true to its own past tradition the Catholic church today ought to put its educational resources at the service of a wider community. The young parent beginning a family, the middle aged person coping with change of life or the old person facing retirement, all have a claim upon the church's educational concern.

The church has more than enough real estate in the cities, in suburbia and in rural lands. Where old churches exist in cities, they could easily become educational centers. If anything new is to be built by the churches, the buildings should be multi-purpose from the start. The construction of expensive schools that are used for a few hours a week is scandalous. Even erecting buildings that are used for nothing but churches ought to be seriously questioned. Something other than niggardliness might lead one to advocate a moratorium on church construction. A community may indeed need a local gathering point but such a building ought to be a community kind and not a box-like structure looking like what churches are supposed to look like. The liturgy ought to be celebrated as an overflow of a community's concern with education and social change. The churches are never going to do much until they dynamite the assumption that religious education is what the children get while the adults go to worship service. Despite tactical changes in this area, neither Catholic nor Protestant churches have made much progress in challenging this long-standing arrangement.

Anyone who proposes to change the church's education in the direction I have called adult centered should not expect immediate and sensational results. It will take many years to establish the church's credibility in its claim to be interested in the education of the whole community. The tenuousness of the educational structure to carry through the reform only makes it imperative that there be a concerted drive in this direction. Canon F. Drinkwater, one of the grand old gentlemen of this movement, has pointed out that it is only in the twentieth century that the church has had the social institutions to begin trying to give every Christian an adult theology.[15] In religious education we are still in the Age of the Fathers. We have a long way to go but no one should be surprised that our success up to now has been limited. Our opportunities are only beginning.

15. F. H. Drinkwater, *Telling the Good News* (London, 1960), p. 102.